THIS BOOK BELONGS TO:

CHRISTMAS 2005

25th Anniversary Edition

Christmas
with **Southern Living**
2005

25th Anniversary Edition

Christmas
with Southern Living
2005

Edited by Rebecca Brennan and Julie Gunter

Oxmoor House®

©2005 by Oxmoor House, Inc.
Book Division of Southern Progress Corporation
P. O. Box 2262, Birmingham, Alabama 35201-2262

Southern Living® is a federally registered trademark belonging to
Southern Living, Inc.

ISBN: 0-8487-3014-3
ISSN: 0747-7791
Library of Congress Control Number: 2005925529
Printed in the United States of America
First Printing 2005

Editor in Chief: Nancy Fitzpatrick Wyatt
Executive Editor: Susan Carlisle Payne
Art Director: Cynthia Rose Cooper
Copy Chief: Allison Long Lowery

Christmas with Southern Living® 2005

Editor: Rebecca Brennan
Foods Editor: Julie Gunter
Copy Editors: Donna Baldone, L. Amanda Owens
Editorial Assistant: Jessica Dorsey Kohls
Senior Designer: Melissa Jones Clark
Senior Photographer: Jim Bathie
Senior Photo Stylist: Kay E. Clarke
Photo Stylist: Amy Wilson
Illustrator: Kelly Davis
Director, Test Kitchens: Elizabeth Tyler Luckett
Assistant Director, Test Kitchens: Julie Christopher
Test Kitchens Staff: Kristi Carter, Nicole Lee Faber, Kathleen Royal Phillips,
    Elise Weis, Kelley Self Wilton
Publishing Systems Administrator: Rick Tucker
Director of Production: Phillip Lee
Books Production Manager: Greg A. Amason
Production Assistant: Faye Porter Bonner

Contributors
Indexer: Mary Ann Laurens
Interns: Leighton Batte, Julie Boston, Marian Cairns, Elizabeth Grezaffi, Ashley Lanier

Cover: Spiced Eggnog Pound Cake, page 144
Back cover, clockwise from top left: Hazelnut-Eggnog Punch, page 141; Food Gifts &
Wrapping Ideas, page 158; Pecan Biscotti, page 24; Christmas Cottage Charm, page 74

Crab and Oyster Bisque
Cabbage and Apple Salad
with Roasted Onions
Coffee-Crusted Beef Wellingtons
Cast-Iron Herbed Potatoes Anna
Carrots with Country Bacon
Scalloped Greens
Chocolate Tiramisù Charlotte
Cardamom-Scented Sweet Potato Pie
Wine   Coffee

contents

Welcome to Our
Christmas with Southern Living
25th Anniversary Edition

dear friends,

Editor Becky Brennan and I were chatting about this 25th anniversary edition one day, and I got so enthused that Becky let me be the one to welcome you to this year's special edition. The idea to do this book sprang from *Southern Living* magazine readers' passion for Christmas. Everyone knows that holidays hold a special place in the hearts of Southerners. The holiday issues of the magazine are always eagerly anticipated by subscribers and are best sellers on the newsstand. It seemed that there might be an audience for additional great holiday-decorating and gift-giving ideas as well as even more new recipes than the pages of the magazine could offer. So in 1981 the first *Christmas with Southern Living* was published.

The first edition of Christmas with Southern Living *was smaller, squarer, and 140 pages compared with this volume of 192 pages.*

That first edition included a tree that featured ornaments of sweet gum balls studded with nandina berries created by John Floyd, then senior horticulturist and now *Southern Living* magazine editor in chief. Julia Hamilton, then interiors editor and now senior writer, crafted a kitchen wreath from holly and wooden spoons. Van Chaplin, John O'Hagan, and Charles Walton—all *Southern Living* senior photographers today—contributed memorable images to the 1981 book and many others throughout the years. Indeed, Charles captured the graphic photo illustration style that framed the covers of the first nine editions. Susan Payne, then foods editor and now executive editor of *Southern Living* books and director of *Christmas with Southern Living*, had a hand in including the now famous Hummingbird Cake in the debut edition.

By the mid-80s, when I had the opportunity to be the editor of *Christmas with Southern Living*, it was a bona fide hit. Now, as my 30-year anniversary with this company approaches, I realize that this publication is a holiday tradition in itself. My mother collected every edition of this Christmas book and gave it or *Southern Living Annual Recipes* to her family and friends every year. Our family holiday dinners always included some of

See our 25th Anniversary Favorites, featuring the best-ever recipes, wreaths, and cakes, starting on page 10.

Twenty-five volumes, 3,916 pages, 3,942 photos, 2,010 recipes, more ideas than we can count, and millions of copies later, we thank you for making *Christmas with Southern Living* a part of your holiday tradition.

the latest new recipes from *Christmas with Southern Living*. My mother was a wonderful cook and taught me to love cooking, too. My recollections of cooking by Mom's side in her cozy kitchen, setting the table with her best china and silver that we polished together, and enjoying the glorious spread of heavenly dishes always brings her close to me. I'm sure that's a memory I share with thousands of Southern women. My mother's *Christmas with Southern Living* collection is now on my stepdaughter's shelves. Emily and I share the joy of planning menus, the camaraderie of cooking together, and the immense joy of pleasing our loved ones with memorable meals.

I can't wait to sit down with Em and plan our menus for the holidays from this book's incredible array of ideas and recipes. Some of this year's team have been the creative force behind the book for over 10 years, including editors Becky Brennan and Julie Gunter, photo team Jim Bathie and Kay Clarke, art director Cindy Cooper, and designers Melissa Clark and Emily Parrish. We all wish you and yours the happiest of holidays and hope that *Christmas with Southern Living* is a part of your holidays and sweet memories this year and for years to come.

Nancy

Nancy Wyatt
Editor in Chief
Southern Living Books

25 years ago in 1981...

1. Black-and-white photographs and illustrations punctuated much of *Southern Living* magazine.
2. Ronald Reagan was inaugurated as the 40th President of the United States.
3. Walter Cronkite delivered his final CBS Evening News telecast.
4. "Celebration" by Kool and the Gang and "9 to 5" by Dolly Parton were top singles. Television series *Dynasty* and *Hill Street Blues* premiered. Sissy Spacek won best actress in a leading role for *Coal Miner's Daughter* at the 53rd Annual Academy Awards.
5. Richard Petty won the Nascar Daytona 500.
6. The first-class U.S. letter rate rose from 15 to 18 to 20 cents.
7. The first space shuttle, Columbia,—launched from the Kennedy Space Center in Cape Canaveral, Florida—made 36 Earth orbits and landed at Edwards Air Force Base in Southern California.
8. Prince Charles and Lady Diana Spencer became engaged in February and married in July in London before a worldwide television audience. In November, Buckingham Palace announced that the Princess of Wales was expecting a baby in June 1982.
9. Paul "Bear" Bryant was head football coach at the University of Alabama.
10. The first edition of *Christmas with Southern Living* was published.

25th Anniversary Special Section

With this 25th edition of *Christmas with Southern Living®*, we've gathered our three all-time favorite cooking and decorating collections—ultimate Christmas dishes, layer cakes, and lovely wreaths. It's a fond reflection of 25 years of Southern holiday tradition.

25 All-Time Favorite Christmas Recipes

*These holiday staff favorites are the recipes
we serve our families year after year.*

Butter Coconut Pie, page 18

Grapefruit-Rosemary Daiquiris

Grapefruit-Rosemary Daiquiris

The surprising combo of citrus and herb tastes great in this slushy daiquiri. For a special effect, dip rims of glasses in coarse sugar before filling.

Prep: 17 min.   Cook: 10 min.   Other: 8 hrs.

3   cups freshly squeezed ruby red grapefruit juice
    (about 7 grapefruit)
1½ cups water
⅔   cup sugar
2   large sprigs fresh rosemary
⅓   cup vodka (optional)
1½ teaspoons finely chopped fresh rosemary
Sparkling white sugar (optional)
Garnish: fresh rosemary sprigs

Pour 2½ cups grapefruit juice into 2 ice cube trays; freeze until firm. Cover and chill remaining juice.

Stir together water, sugar, and 2 rosemary sprigs in a saucepan; bring to a boil. Cover, reduce heat, and simmer 10 minutes. Remove from heat; discard rosemary sprigs. Cool syrup; chill.

Process frozen juice cubes, remaining ½ cup grapefruit juice, rosemary syrup, vodka, if desired, and chopped rosemary in a 5-cup blender for 10 seconds or until slushy. Serve in sugar-rimmed glasses, and garnish, if desired. Yield: 5 cups.

Fix it Faster: Use 3 cups bottled ruby red grapefruit juice.

Note: For sugared rims, dip rims of stemmed glasses into a thin coating of light corn syrup or water, and then spin rims in a plateful of sparkling white sugar.

Savory Kalamata Cheesecake Squares

Savory Kalamata Cheesecake Squares

Garnish your platter with herbs and olives so your guests will know this is an appetizer and not dessert. Serve a Pinot Noir with these rich squares.

Prep: 29 min.   Cook: 32 min.   Other: 1 hr.

1¼ cups Italian-seasoned breadcrumbs
½ cup very finely chopped pecans
⅓ cup butter or margarine, melted
1 (8-ounce) package cream cheese, softened
1 (3-ounce) package cream cheese, softened
1 (8-ounce) container sour cream
1 tablespoon all-purpose flour
¼ teaspoon salt
¼ teaspoon pepper
1 large egg
1 egg yolk
½ cup pitted kalamata olives, sliced or chopped
1 tablespoon chopped fresh rosemary
Garnishes: fresh rosemary sprigs, kalamata olives

Combine first 3 ingredients; stir well. Press crumb mixture firmly into a lightly greased, foil-lined 9" square pan. Bake at 350° for 12 minutes; set aside to cool.

Meanwhile, beat cream cheese, sour cream, and next 3 ingredients at medium speed with an electric mixer until smooth. Add egg and egg yolk, beating just until blended. Stir in olives and rosemary; pour filling into baked crust.

Bake at 350° for 20 minutes or just until firm; cool to room temperature on a wire rack. Cover and chill at least 1 hour.

To serve, lift foil out of pan, and cut cheesecake into little squares. Garnish serving platter, if desired. Store in refrigerator. Yield: 3 dozen.

The **rich and fruity flavor** of a kalamata olive is hard to top.

editor's favorite

Butternut Squash Spread on Cheese Croutons

Baked butternut squash and Asiago cheese blend with herbs and toasted pecans for a fabulous-tasting spread.

Prep: 22 min.   Cook: 1hr., 6 min.

1   medium butternut squash (about 2 pounds)
3   tablespoons butter or margarine
3   garlic cloves, minced
½   (8-ounce) package cream cheese, softened
1½ cups freshly grated Asiago cheese, divided
1   tablespoon sugar
½   cup toasted chopped pecans
2   teaspoons chopped fresh thyme
2   teaspoons chopped fresh rosemary
1   baguette, cut into 48 thin slices
½   cup olive oil
Salt and pepper
Garnish: small sprigs of fresh thyme

Microwave squash on HIGH 1 to 2 minutes. (This step softens squash for slicing.) Cut squash in half lengthwise; remove and discard seeds. Place squash, cut sides down, in a 13" x 9" baking dish. Add hot water to dish to depth of 1". Bake, uncovered, at 350° for 1 hour or until squash is very tender. Let cool slightly.

Scoop out squash pulp. Mash pulp, and place in a large bowl.

Melt butter in a small skillet over medium-high heat. Add garlic; sauté 1 minute. Add garlic butter to squash pulp in bowl. Add cream cheese, ½ cup Asiago cheese, and sugar; beat at medium speed with an electric mixer until smooth. Stir in pecans and chopped herbs.

Place baguette slices on 2 large ungreased baking sheets; brush or drizzle with olive oil. Sprinkle slices with salt and pepper. Bake at 400° for 4 minutes. Sprinkle slices with remaining 1 cup Asiago cheese. Bake 2 more minutes or until cheese melts.

Spoon 1 tablespoon squash mixture onto each cheese crouton. Garnish, if desired. Yield: 4 dozen.

make ahead • editor's favorite

Florentine Artichoke Dip

Make this dip ahead, and bake it just before serving. Crisp bagel chips make great dippers.

Prep: 30 min.   Cook: 25 min.

1   (10-ounce) package frozen chopped spinach, thawed
2   (6-ounce) jars marinated artichoke hearts, drained and chopped
1½ (8-ounce) packages cream cheese, softened
1   cup freshly shredded Parmesan cheese
½   cup mayonnaise
3   large garlic cloves, pressed
2   tablespoons lemon juice
1½ cups French breadcrumbs (homemade; see Note)
2   tablespoons butter or margarine, melted

Drain spinach; press between layers of paper towels to remove excess moisture.

Combine spinach, artichoke hearts, and next 5 ingredients in a bowl, stirring well. Spoon into a greased 11" x 7" baking dish. Combine breadcrumbs and butter; sprinkle over spinach mixture.

Bake, uncovered, at 375° for 25 minutes or until browned. Serve with bagel chips, crackers, or breadsticks. Yield: 4 cups.

Note: To get 1½ cups French breadcrumbs, tear off a piece of a baguette. Pulse in a food processor until coarse crumbs form. Measure crumbs, tear off another chunk, and repeat procedure until you get 1½ cups.

❄ *make ahead*
Grapefruit Compote in Rosemary Syrup

If you have an abundance of grapefruit during the holidays, this recipe is a great use for it.

Prep: 20 min.   Cook: 5 min.

1	cup sugar
½	cup water
3	tablespoons honey
3	sprigs fresh rosemary
6	large grapefruit
½	cup maraschino cherries with stems

Garnish: fresh rosemary sprigs

Combine first 4 ingredients in a saucepan; bring to a boil over medium heat. Boil 5 minutes. Remove from heat, and let cool completely. Remove and discard rosemary.

Section grapefruit over a large bowl, catching juices. Pour rosemary syrup over fruit in bowl. Add cherries. Cover and chill until ready to serve. Garnish, if desired. Yield: 8 to 10 servings.

Serve in compotes and enjoy the herb-kissed syrup with each spoonful.

Grapefruit Compote in Rosemary Syrup

Rum Fudge Cakes

Rum Fudge Cakes

A wooden spoon gets you from start to finish with this recipe. Rum flavor permeates these petite fudgy cakes that received our highest rating. Make and freeze them ahead.

Prep: 21 min.   Cook: 22 min.   Other: 10 min.

1	cup butter
4	(1-ounce) unsweetened chocolate squares
4	(1-ounce) semisweet chocolate squares
1⅓	cups granulated sugar
⅓	cup heavy whipping cream
1½	teaspoons rum extract
3	large eggs
1	cup all-purpose flour
1	cup (6 ounces) semisweet chocolate mini-morsels

Powdered sugar

Melt butter and chocolate squares in a heavy saucepan over medium-low heat, stirring often. Remove from heat, and cool completely. Stir in granulated sugar, whipping cream, and rum extract until blended. Add eggs, 1 at a time, stirring until blended after each addition. Gently fold in flour. Stir in mini-morsels.

Spoon batter into lightly greased miniature (1¾") muffin pans, filling almost full.

Bake at 375° for 14 minutes or until a wooden pick inserted in center comes out almost clean. Let cool in pans on wire racks 10 minutes. Remove to wire racks to cool completely. Sprinkle cakes with powdered sugar before serving. Yield: 4 dozen.

*Coffee Lovers'
Coffee Cake*

a pastry blender until crumbly. Press half of crumb mixture into a lightly greased 9" square pan; set aside.

Combine sour cream and baking soda, stirring well. Add to remaining crumb mixture, stirring just until dry ingredients are moistened. Add egg, stirring gently to combine. Pour sour cream mixture over crumb crust in pan; sprinkle with pecans.

Bake at 350° for 45 minutes. Cool and cut into squares. Yield: 1 (9") coffee cake.

❄editor's favorite • gift idea

Butter Coconut Pie

This easy coconut pie makes a nice gift packaged in the disposable pan it's baked in. Crimp the store-bought crust's edges to make it look homemade. See photo on page 12.

Prep: 15 min.   Cook: 50 min.   Other: 15 min.

1   (9") frozen deep-dish pastry shell (we tested with
    Mrs. Smith's)
1   cup sugar
1   tablespoon all-purpose flour
3   large eggs, lightly beaten
1   (3.5-ounce) can sweetened flaked coconut
½   cup evaporated milk
⅓   cup butter, melted
1   teaspoon vanilla extract
Garnish: toasted flaked coconut

Remove frozen pastry shell from package; let stand at room temperature 15 minutes. Smooth edges of pastry shell, and crimp.

Line pastry with aluminum foil or parchment paper, and fill with dried beans or pie weights. Bake at 400° for 8 to 10 minutes or until lightly browned. Remove weights and foil.

Combine sugar and flour in a large bowl; stir in eggs. Add 1 can coconut and next 3 ingredients, stirring well. Pour filling into prepared piecrust.

Bake at 325° for 40 minutes or until pie is just set (center will be slightly jiggly). Cool completely. Store in refrigerator. Garnish, if desired. Yield: 1 (9") pie.

Note: You can use half of a 15-ounce package of refrigerated piecrusts and a 9" pieplate instead of a frozen piecrust. The filling will be more shallow and crust may need shielding to prevent overbrowning.

❄make ahead • editor's favorite

Coffee Lovers' Coffee Cake

A buttery coffee crumb mixture makes a shortbreadlike crust for this easy snack cake.

Prep: 17 min.   Cook: 45 min.

2   cups all-purpose flour
2   teaspoons instant coffee granules
2   cups firmly packed light brown sugar
1   teaspoon ground cinnamon
½   teaspoon salt
½   cup butter or margarine, cut into pieces
1   (8-ounce) container sour cream
1   teaspoon baking soda
1   large egg, lightly beaten
1   cup chopped pecans or walnuts

Combine flour and coffee granules in a large bowl. Add brown sugar, cinnamon, and salt; stir well. Cut in butter with

make ahead • editor's favorite

Eggnog Pie

Prep: 17 min.   Cook: 26 min.   Other: 4 hrs., 6 min.

2   cups pecan shortbread cookie crumbs (about 18 cookies; we tested with Pecan Sandies)

¼   cup butter or margarine, melted

½   cup semisweet chocolate morsels

2¼   cups whipping cream

⅓   cup granulated sugar

½   cup bourbon or rum

½   teaspoon freshly grated nutmeg

1   envelope unflavored gelatin

¼   cup cold water

6   egg yolks, lightly beaten

1   tablespoon butter or margarine

Freshly grated nutmeg

Powdered sugar

Unsweetened whipped cream (optional)

Stir together cookie crumbs and ¼ cup melted butter; press firmly into a greased 9" deep-dish pieplate. Bake at 350° for 8 minutes. Remove crust from oven, and sprinkle chocolate morsels into warm crust. Let stand 5 minutes or until morsels melt; carefully spread chocolate over bottom of crust with a spatula. Set aside.

Stir together whipping cream and next 3 ingredients in top of a double boiler; bring water just to a simmer. Cook over simmering water 6 to 8 minutes or until thoroughly heated.

Meanwhile, sprinkle gelatin over cold water in a small bowl; let stand 1 minute.

Gradually whisk one-fourth of warm cream mixture into egg yolks. Add to remaining warm cream, whisking constantly. Whisk in softened gelatin. Cook over simmering water 3 to 5 minutes or until custard reaches 160°. Remove from heat; add 1 tablespoon butter, stirring gently until butter melts. Cool filling to room temperature.

Pour filling into prepared crust. Gently cover with plastic wrap, pressing directly on surface of filling. Chill pie at least 4 hours or until firm.

Sprinkle nutmeg and powdered sugar over pie before serving. Serve with dollops of whipped cream and more nutmeg, if desired. Store pie in refrigerator. Yield: 1 (9") pie.

Note: The chocolate layer will harden as the pie chills in the refrigerator. Use a sharp knife and gentle pressure to slice pie.

This dessert's like a "black bottom" eggnog pie.

Eggnog Pie

Hot Fudge Cheesecake

This chocoholic's dessert develops a brownielike top as it bakes. Serve leftover Hot Fudge Sauce over ice cream, pound cake, or as fondue.

Prep: 28 min. Cook: 1hr., 8 min. Other: 30 min.

1	cup crushed saltine crackers
½	cup finely chopped walnuts
6	tablespoons butter or margarine, melted
3	tablespoons sugar
6	(1-ounce) semisweet chocolate squares
¾	cup butter or margarine
1	(8-ounce) package cream cheese, softened
¾	cup sugar
3	large eggs

Hot Fudge Sauce
Garnish: walnut halves

Combine first 4 ingredients; stir well. Firmly press onto bottom and 2½" up sides of a lightly greased 7" springform pan. Bake at 350° for 8 minutes. Remove to a wire rack; let cool. Reduce oven temperature to 300°.

Combine chocolate squares and ¾ cup butter in a heavy saucepan. Cook over medium-low heat until mixture is melted and smooth, stirring often. Remove from heat, and let cool.

Hot Fudge Cheesecake

Beat cream cheese at medium speed with an electric mixer until creamy. Add ¾ cup sugar; beat well. Add eggs, 1 at a time, beating after each addition. Stir in cooled chocolate mixture. Pour into prepared crust.

Bake at 300° for 50 minutes to 1 hour or until almost set. Turn oven off. Let cheesecake cool in oven 30 minutes. Remove to a wire rack; let cool to room temperature.

Remove sides of pan. Serve cheesecake with Hot Fudge Sauce. Garnish, if desired. Yield: 8 to 10 servings.

hot fudge sauce

Prep: 5 min. Cook: 7 min.

1	(12-ounce) package semisweet chocolate morsels
1	cup half-and-half
1	tablespoon butter or margarine
1	teaspoon vanilla extract

Combine chocolate morsels and half-and-half in a heavy saucepan. Cook over medium heat until chocolate melts and mixture is smooth, stirring frequently. Remove from heat; stir in butter and vanilla. Serve warm. Yield: 2 cups.

Frozen Pistachio Cheesecake

No cracks to worry about with this luscious cheesecake; it's frozen, not baked.

Prep: 30 min. Cook: 12 min. Other: 6 hrs.

1	cup pistachio nuts
1	cup sugar cookie crumbs (16 cookies; we tested with Pepperidge Farm Bordeaux cookies)
3	tablespoons granulated sugar
⅓	cup butter or margarine, melted
⅔	cup whipping cream
12	ounces white chocolate, finely chopped
4	(8-ounce) packages cream cheese, softened
½	cup butter or margarine, softened
⅔	cup sifted powdered sugar
2	teaspoons vanilla extract

Garnish: additional pistachio nuts

Position knife blade in food processor bowl; add 1 cup pistachio nuts. Process until chopped. Add cookie crumbs, 3 tablespoons sugar, and melted butter. Pulse 4 or 5 times or until blended. Press crumb mixture onto bottom and 1½" up

sides of a lightly greased 9" springform pan. Bake crust at 350° for 12 minutes or until lightly browned. Cool completely on a wire rack.

Bring whipping cream to a simmer in a heavy saucepan over medium heat. Remove from heat, and add chopped white chocolate. Let stand 2 to 3 minutes. Stir gently with a rubber spatula until smooth.

Beat cream cheese and softened butter at medium speed with an electric mixer until creamy. Add powdered sugar,

and beat until light and fluffy. Add melted white chocolate mixture and vanilla; beat 3 minutes or until very smooth. Pour batter into prepared crust. Cover and freeze until firm or up to 1 week.

Let stand at room temperature about 30 minutes before serving or until easy to slice. Remove sides of pan. Garnish cheesecake, if desired. Cut frozen cheesecake with a sharp knife, dipping knife in hot water and wiping it dry between each slice. Yield: 10 to 12 servings.

Double Chocolate Espresso Brownies

Wow your holiday dinner guests with a
tower of brownie cutouts. Drizzle with
fudge sauce and use tongs for serving.

Double Chocolate Espresso Brownies

Savor the combination of coffee and chocolate in these luscious brownies.

Prep: 40 min.   Cook: 50 min.   Other: 2 hrs.

1¼ cups all-purpose flour
¼ teaspoon baking soda
⅛ teaspoon baking powder
⅛ teaspoon salt
14 (1-ounce) semisweet chocolate squares, finely chopped
1 cup sugar
½ cup butter or margarine
¼ cup light corn syrup
¼ cup brewed espresso or French roast coffee
3 large eggs
1 tablespoon vanilla extract
1 cup coarsely chopped walnuts
6 ounces premium Swiss dark chocolate or milk chocolate, coarsely chopped

Coat a 13" x 9" pan with cooking spray. Line pan with aluminum foil, allowing ends to hang over short sides of pan. Tuck overlapping ends under rim on short sides. Coat foil with cooking spray; set pan aside.

Combine flour and next 3 ingredients in a small bowl. Place chopped semisweet chocolate in a large bowl; set bowls aside.

Combine sugar and next 3 ingredients in a saucepan. Cook over medium heat, stirring constantly, until sugar and butter melt and mixture comes to a rolling boil. Remove from heat, and pour over chopped chocolate in bowl; let stand 2 minutes (do not stir).

Beat at low speed with an electric mixer until chocolate melts and mixture is smooth. Add eggs, 1 at a time, beating well after each addition. Add flour mixture; beat at medium speed until well blended. Stir in vanilla, walnuts, and dark chocolate.

Spoon batter into prepared pan, spreading evenly.

Bake at 325° for 38 to 40 minutes. Cool completely in pan on a wire rack. Cover and chill at least 2 hours.

Carefully invert brownies from pan, using overlapping foil as handles; remove foil. Invert brownies again onto a cutting board; cut into squares or circles. (We used a 2½" round cutter. There'll be some fudgy scraps left for nibbling or topping with ice cream.) Yield: 4 dozen.

White Chocolate, Peanut, and Caramel Candy Cookies

These yummy drop cookies have more than the typical amount of chunks of candy and nuts. For this recipe, chilling the dough twice really helps cookies hold a plump shape during baking. See photo on page 7.

Prep: 41 min.   Cook: 11 min. per batch

1 cup butter, softened
1 cup granulated sugar
1 cup firmly packed light brown sugar
2 large eggs
1 teaspoon vanilla extract
2½ cups uncooked regular oats
2 cups all-purpose flour
1 teaspoon baking powder
½ teaspoon baking soda
½ teaspoon salt
3 (1.7-ounce) packages chocolate-covered caramel candies, chilled and chopped (we tested with Rolo)
2 (4-ounce) white chocolate bars, chopped (we tested with Ghirardelli)
1½ cups unsalted peanuts, chopped

Beat butter at medium speed with an electric mixer until creamy; add sugars, beating well. Add eggs and vanilla, beating until blended.

Process oats in a blender or food processor until finely ground. Combine oats, flour, and next 3 ingredients; add to butter mixture, beating well. Stir in chopped candy, white chocolate, and peanuts. Chill dough 1 hour, if desired.

Shape dough into 1½" balls, and place on lightly greased or parchment paper-lined baking sheets. Chill briefly, if desired. Bake at 375° for 10 to 11 minutes or until lightly browned. Cool 1 minute on baking sheets. Remove to wire racks to cool. Yield: 5½ dozen.

Butter-Nut Truffles

chute until mixture is smooth, stopping to scrape down sides. Add butter and nut flavoring; process until blended. Transfer mixture to a bowl; stir in chopped candy bars. Cover and chill 30 minutes.

Shape chocolate mixture into 1" balls; roll in finely crushed candy bars. Store truffles in refrigerator up to 1 week. Let stand at room temperature briefly before serving. Yield: about 2½ dozen.

❄️editor's favorite • make ahead • gift idea
Pecan Biscotti
Cornmeal adds an unusual twist to these crunchy cookies.

Prep: 23 min.   Cook: 39 min.   Other: 10 min.

1¾ cups all-purpose flour
½   cup yellow cornmeal
1¼ teaspoons baking powder
¼   teaspoon salt
1   cup finely chopped pecans, toasted
2   large eggs, lightly beaten
¾   cup sugar
½   cup vegetable oil
¼   teaspoon almond extract or vanilla extract

Combine first 5 ingredients in a large bowl.

Stir together eggs and remaining 3 ingredients; gradually add to flour mixture, stirring just until dry ingredients are moistened.

Divide dough in half. With lightly floured hands, shape each portion into a 12" x 2" log. Place logs 3" apart on a lightly greased baking sheet.

Bake at 350° for 25 minutes. Cool logs on baking sheet 10 minutes.

Cut each log diagonally into ¾"-thick slices with a serrated knife, using a gentle sawing motion. Return slices, cut side down, to baking sheet.

Bake at 350° for 7 minutes. Turn biscotti over, and bake 7 more minutes. Remove to wire racks to cool completely. Yield: 2½ dozen.

❄️make ahead • editor's favorite • gift idea
Butter-Nut Truffles
You'll recognize a crispy, chocolaty candy bar in the filling and coating for these bittersweet truffles.

Prep: 44 min.   Other: 30 min.

5   (2.1-ounce) chocolate-covered crispy peanut-buttery candy bars, frozen (we tested with Butterfinger)
2   (4-ounce) bittersweet chocolate baking bars, broken into pieces (we tested with Ghirardelli)
3   tablespoons whipping cream
3   tablespoons butter or margarine
½   teaspoon butter and nut flavoring

Break 2 candy bars into pieces. Process candy bar pieces in a food processor until finely crushed. Place on a shallow plate; set aside. Chop remaining 3 candy bars; set aside.

Place bittersweet chocolate in food processor bowl, and pulse until finely chopped.

Combine whipping cream and butter in a 1-cup glass measuring cup; microwave on HIGH 1 minute or until butter is melted and cream begins to boil. With processor running, slowly pour hot cream and butter through food

Pecan Biscotti

*Apple-Berry Cobbler with
Vanilla Bean Hard Sauce*

Apple-Berry Cobbler with Vanilla Bean Hard Sauce

A combination of apple varieties gives this cobbler depth of flavor.

Prep: 17 min.   Cook: 50 min.

4   baking apples (about 1¾ pounds), peeled, cored, and sliced (we tested with Braeburn and Granny Smith apples)
2   cups fresh or frozen cranberries, partially thawed
1   cup firmly packed light brown sugar
½   teaspoon ground cinnamon
2   teaspoons cornstarch
¼   cup water
1   cup all-purpose flour
½   cup toasted wheat germ
1   teaspoon baking powder
¼   teaspoon salt
½   cup butter or margarine, softened
½   cup granulated sugar
1½ tablespoons milk
1   large egg
1   teaspoon vanilla extract
Vanilla Bean Hard Sauce

Toss together first 4 ingredients in large bowl. Combine cornstarch and water; stir into apple-cranberry mixture. Spoon apple-cranberry mixture into a greased 11" x 7" baking dish. Cover and set aside.

Combine flour and next 3 ingredients; set aside.

Beat butter at medium speed with an electric mixer until creamy. Gradually add ½ cup sugar, beating well. Add milk, egg, and vanilla, beating well. Stir in flour mixture.

Drop batter by spoonfuls over apple-cranberry mixture. Bake, uncovered, at 350° for 50 minutes or until golden and bubbly. Serve hot with Vanilla Bean Hard Sauce or vanilla ice cream. Yield: 8 servings.

vanilla bean hard sauce

Prep: 8 min.

1   vanilla bean, split lengthwise
1   cup butter, softened
2   cups sifted powdered sugar

Scrape seeds from vanilla bean into mixing bowl with butter. Beat butter at medium speed with electric mixer until creamy. Gradually add sugar, beating well. Cover and chill until ready to serve. Soften slightly before serving. Yield: 1⅔ cups.

Note: One 6" vanilla bean equals about 1 tablespoon vanilla extract if you want to substitute extract.

Vanilla bean gets star billing in this speckled hard sauce.

Beef Tenderloin with Shallot Sauce

Beef Tenderloin with Shallot Sauce

Marsala wine and charred shallots impart a rich and smoky essence to this tenderloin's deep brown sauce.

Prep: 25 min.   Cook: 57 min.

1	pound shallots, peeled and halved lengthwise
2	tablespoons olive oil
¾	teaspoon salt
½	teaspoon pepper
1	tablespoon salt
1½	teaspoons onion powder
1½	teaspoons garlic powder
1½	teaspoons pepper
1½	teaspoons chopped fresh thyme or ½ teaspoon dried thyme
1	(8-pound) beef tenderloin, trimmed (see Note)
¼	cup olive oil
3	cups beef broth
1	cup dry Marsala wine
2	tablespoons all-purpose flour
3	tablespoons water
3	tablespoons butter or margarine
¼	teaspoon pepper

Garnish: fresh thyme

Toss shallots and 2 tablespoons oil in a bowl; stir in ¾ teaspoon salt and ½ teaspoon pepper. Set aside.

Stir together 1 tablespoon salt and next 4 ingredients. Rub tenderloin with ¼ cup olive oil; sprinkle seasonings over top and sides of tenderloin, pressing gently with fingers. Place tenderloin in a large lightly greased roasting pan; arrange shallots around tenderloin.

Bake, uncovered, at 500° for 25 minutes. Reduce oven temperature to 375°, and bake 15 to 20 minutes or until a meat thermometer inserted into thickest part of tenderloin registers 145° (medium-rare) or 160° (medium).

Meanwhile, stir together beef broth and Marsala in a large skillet. Bring to a boil; boil 8 minutes or until liquid is reduced to 2 cups.

Remove tenderloin to a serving platter, and cover with aluminum foil; reserve shallots and drippings in pan. Add broth reduction to pan, and place over medium heat on cooktop, stirring to loosen particles from bottom of pan.

Whisk together flour and water until smooth; stir into sauce in roasting pan. Cook over medium heat 3 minutes, or until sauce is slightly thickened, stirring constantly. Add butter, stirring just until melted. Stir in ¼ teaspoon pepper. Thinly slice tenderloin, and serve with sauce. Garnish, if desired. Yield: 16 servings.

Note: Find beef tenderloin sealed in plastic in the meat section of your supermarket. Once you trim the tenderloin you should yield about 6 pounds of meat. To save time, ask your butcher to trim it for you.

Tawny Baked Ham

A smoky, sweet aroma will fill your kitchen as this big ham bakes.

Prep: 15 min.   Cook: 2½ hrs.   Other: 10 min.

1	(19-pound) smoked, fully cooked whole ham
35	whole cloves (2 teaspoons)
⅓	cup Dijon mustard
1	cup firmly packed light brown sugar
2	cups apple cider
2	cups pitted whole dates
2	cups dried figs, stems removed
2	cups pitted prunes
2	cups tawny port wine

Garnishes: kumquats, dried figs, apples

Remove and discard skin from ham. Make ⅛"-deep cuts in fat on ham in a diamond design. Using a metal skewer, make a hole in center of each diamond. Insert a clove into each hole. Brush mustard over top and sides of ham. Coat ham with brown sugar, pressing into mustard, if necessary.

Place ham, fat side up, in a lightly greased large shallow roasting pan. Insert a meat thermometer, making sure it does not touch fat or bone. Pour apple cider into pan.

Bake, uncovered, at 350° for 2 hours, basting often with apple cider.

Combine dates and next 3 ingredients; pour into pan with ham. Bake 30 minutes or until meat thermometer registers 140°, basting often with mixture in pan; cover ham with aluminum foil, if necessary, to prevent burning.

Transfer ham to a serving platter; let stand 10 minutes before slicing. Remove fruit from pan, using a slotted spoon.

Pour pan drippings into a large saucepan. Strain fat, if desired. Cook over medium-high heat 5 minutes or until reduced by half. Stir in reserved fruit. Serve sauce with ham. Garnish, if desired. Yield: 35 servings.

Seasoned Roast Turkey

Nine spices season this bird that yields drippings for some dynamite gravy.

Prep: 18 min.   Cook: 3½ hrs.   Other: 15 min.

1   (12- to 14-pound) fresh or frozen turkey, thawed
1   tablespoon salt
2   teaspoons seasoned salt
1   teaspoon ground black pepper
1   teaspoon poultry seasoning
1   teaspoon garlic powder
1   teaspoon paprika
1   teaspoon ground red pepper
1   teaspoon dried basil
½   teaspoon ground ginger
2   tablespoons butter or margarine, softened
1   cup water
Giblet Gravy
Garnishes: red grapes, Seckel pears

Remove giblets and neck from turkey; reserve for making Giblet Gravy, if desired. Rinse turkey with cold water; pat dry. Place turkey, breast side up, in a lightly greased broiler pan or roasting pan.

Combine salt and next 8 ingredients. Using fingers, carefully loosen skin from turkey at neck area, working down to breast and thigh area. Rub about one-third of seasonings under skin. Rub skin with softened butter; rub with remaining seasonings. Tie legs together with heavy string, or tuck under flap of skin. Lift wing tips up and over back; tuck under turkey.

Add water to pan. Cover turkey with aluminum foil. Bake at 325° for 3 to 3½ hours or until a meat thermometer inserted into meaty part of thigh registers 180°, uncovering turkey after 2 hours. Transfer turkey to a serving platter, reserving pan drippings for gravy. Let turkey stand 15 minutes before carving. Garnish, if desired. Yield: 12 to 14 servings.

Note: Remember to allow about 3 days for a 12- to 14-pound frozen turkey to thaw in the refrigerator. And be sure to hunt down your carving set well before Christmas day. Sharpen carving knife, if needed.

giblet gravy

A long-simmering broth and pan drippings contribute rich flavor to this abundant gravy that's not overly thick.

Prep: 5 min.   Cook: 2 hrs., 10 min.

Neck and giblets reserved from turkey
4   cups water
1   celery rib with leaves, cut into pieces
1   medium onion, quartered
½   cup all-purpose flour
½   cup water
½   teaspoon salt
1   teaspoon pepper

Combine first 4 ingredients in a large saucepan. Bring to a boil; cover, reduce heat, and simmer 2 hours, removing liver after 20 minutes to prevent overcooking. Remove from heat. Pour broth through a wire-mesh strainer into a bowl. Remove neck meat from bone; chop and set aside. Chop remaining giblets, and set aside.

Stir 3½ cups broth into reserved turkey drippings in pan that turkey roasted in, or in a large saucepan. Bring to a boil. Combine flour and ½ cup water, stirring until smooth; gradually whisk into boiling broth. Add salt and pepper. Reduce heat to medium, and cook, whisking constantly, 5 minutes or until thickened. Stir in chopped neck meat and giblets; cook until thoroughly heated. Yield: 6 cups.

Carving the holiday
bird is a rite of passage.

Leslie's Favorite Chicken-and-Wild Rice Casserole

Southern Living reader Leslie Flemister declares this dish *perfect for a big family get-together. Make and freeze the casserole ahead, or make two small casseroles.*

Prep: 57 min.   Cook: 50 min.

2   (6.2-ounce) packages fast-cooking long-grain and wild rice mix
¼   cup butter or margarine
4   celery ribs, chopped
2   medium onions, chopped
2   (8-ounce) cans sliced water chestnuts, drained
5   cups chopped cooked chicken
4   cups (1 pound) shredded Cheddar cheese, divided
2   (10¾-ounce) cans cream of mushroom soup, undiluted
1   (16-ounce) container sour cream
1   cup milk
½   teaspoon salt
½   teaspoon pepper
2   cups soft breadcrumbs (homemade)
1   (2.25-ounce) package sliced almonds, toasted

Prepare rice mixes according to package directions.

Meanwhile, melt butter in a large skillet over medium heat; add celery and onion. Sauté 10 minutes or until tender.

Combine water chestnuts, cooked rice, celery and onion, chicken, 3 cups cheese, and next 5 ingredients in a very large bowl.

Spoon mixture into a lightly greased 15" x 10" baking dish or a 4-quart baking dish. Top casserole with breadcrumbs. Bake, uncovered, at 350° for 35 minutes. Sprinkle with remaining 1 cup cheese and almonds; bake 5 more minutes. Yield: 10 to 12 servings.

Note: You can divide this casserole evenly between 2 (11" x 7") baking dishes. Bake as directed above, or freeze casserole up to 1 month. Remove from freezer, and let stand at room temperature 1 hour. Bake, covered, at 350° for 30 minutes. Uncover casserole, and bake 55 more minutes. Sprinkle with remaining 1 cup cheese and almonds; bake 5 more minutes.

Beet Salad with Curried Walnuts

Roasted beets are the heart of this pretty salad, and curried nuts make a great topping. Prepare the walnuts ahead, and store them in an airtight container. See photo on page 11.

Prep: 22 min.   Cook: 1 hr., 25 min.   Other: 1 hr.

1¼   pounds fresh beets (about 4 medium or 2 large)
1   tablespoon olive oil
2   shallots, minced
¼   cup mirin (rice wine)
2   tablespoons chopped fresh mint
3   tablespoons fresh lemon juice
½   teaspoon salt
1   tablespoon butter or margarine
1   tablespoon sugar
1   tablespoon water
1   teaspoon curry powder
¼   teaspoon salt
1   cup walnut halves
3   cups arugula, watercress, or other greens
1   tablespoon olive oil

Trim beets, leaving roots and 1" stems. Scrub beets with a vegetable brush. Drizzle beets with 1 tablespoon olive oil. Place beets in a small roasting pan or cast-iron skillet.

Roast at 425° for 1 hour and 15 to 25 minutes or until tender. Cool beets slightly; trim ends, and rub off skins. Cut beets into 1" chunks.

Combine shallot and next 4 ingredients in a large bowl; add beets, and toss well. Cover and chill 1 hour.

Melt butter in a skillet over medium heat. Add sugar and next 3 ingredients, stirring well to dissolve sugar. Add walnuts, stirring well to coat. Remove from heat.

Spread walnuts in a single layer on a lightly greased jelly-roll pan. Bake at 325° for 15 minutes, stirring twice. Toss well to coat. Cool completely.

Toss arugula and 1 tablespoon olive oil. Divide arugula evenly among 6 salad plates; top evenly with beet salad and curried walnuts. Yield: 6 servings.

Fix it Faster: Forego the roasted beets and use canned or jarred beets.

Sweet Potato-Peanut Soup
with Ham Croutons

Process potato mixture, in batches, in a food processor or blender until smooth. Return potato mixture to Dutch oven; stir in peanut butter. Cook over medium-low heat until soup is smooth, stirring often. Stir in whipping cream, salt, and pepper; cook until thoroughly heated.

To serve, ladle soup into individual bowls. Top each serving with ham. Garnish, if desired. Yield: 10 cups.

editor's favorite • make ahead

Roasted Sweet Potato Salad

Prep: 18 min.   Cook: 45 min.

4   large sweet potatoes, peeled and cubed
2   tablespoons olive oil, divided
¼   cup honey
3   tablespoons white wine vinegar
2   tablespoons chopped fresh rosemary
½   teaspoon salt
½   teaspoon freshly ground pepper
2   garlic cloves, minced
Garnish: fresh rosemary

Coat a large roasting pan with cooking spray; toss together sweet potato and 1 tablespoon oil in pan.

Bake, uncovered, at 450° for 40 to 45 minutes or until sweet potato is tender and roasted, stirring after 30 minutes.

Whisk together remaining 1 tablespoon oil, honey, and next 5 ingredients in a serving bowl. Add warm potato, and toss gently. Cool. Garnish, if desired. Yield: 6 to 8 servings.

editor's favorite

Sweet Potato-Peanut Soup with Ham Croutons

Peanut flavor in this thick, rich appetizer soup comes from creamy peanut butter. The crisp ham croutons are addictive.

Prep: 23 min.   Cook: 45 min.

¼   cup butter or margarine
1   medium onion, chopped
¾   cup chopped celery
2   garlic cloves, chopped
6   cups chicken broth
3   pounds sweet potatoes, peeled and coarsely chopped
1   tablespoon chopped fresh rosemary
2   cups cubed cooked ham
⅔   cup creamy peanut butter
1   cup whipping cream
1   teaspoon salt
¼   teaspoon freshly ground pepper
Garnish: fresh rosemary sprigs

Melt butter in a Dutch oven over medium heat; add onion, celery, and garlic, and sauté 10 minutes or until tender. Add broth, potato, and chopped rosemary. Bring to a boil; cover, reduce heat, and simmer 25 minutes or until potato is very tender.

Meanwhile, heat a large nonstick skillet over medium-high heat. Add ham, and cook until browned and crisp on all sides. Remove from heat; set aside.

Roasted Sweet Potato Salad

Grits Dressing

Spoon grits into a greased 13" x 9" baking dish. Cover and chill until firm. Unmold onto a large cutting board, sliding knife or spatula under grits to loosen them from dish. Cut grits into ¾" cubes. Place in a single layer on a large greased rimmed baking sheet or jellyroll pan.

Bake at 450° for 20 minutes; turn grits, and bake 10 to 12 more minutes or until crisp and browned.

Meanwhile, cook sausage in a large skillet, stirring until it crumbles and is no longer pink; drain.

Melt butter in a large skillet over medium heat; add celery, garlic, and onion. Sauté 5 minutes or until tender. Stir together onion mixture, sausage, and grits croutons, tossing gently. Drizzle egg over mixture; add parsley, stirring gently. Spoon dressing loosely into a greased 11" x 7" baking dish.

Bake, uncovered, at 350° for 35 to 45 minutes or until browned. Yield: 8 servings.

editor's favorite

Green Peas and Baby Limas with Pine Nuts

Fresh rosemary and pine nuts sautéed in butter give these green veggies great flavor.

Prep: 9 min. Cook: 28 min.

1   (14-ounce) can chicken broth
1   (10-ounce) package frozen baby lima beans
4½ cups frozen petite green peas (1½ [16-ounce] packages)
½   teaspoon sugar
¾   cup pine nuts
2   tablespoons butter or margarine, melted
3   green onions, chopped
1   tablespoon chopped fresh rosemary
½   teaspoon salt
¼   teaspoon pepper
3   tablespoons butter or margarine

Bring broth to a boil in a large saucepan; add lima beans. Return to a boil; cover, reduce heat, and simmer 15 minutes or until tender. Stir in peas and ½ teaspoon sugar; cook 2 minutes. Drain.

Sauté pine nuts in 2 tablespoons melted butter in a large skillet over medium heat 2 to 3 minutes or until golden. Add pine nuts to peas and beans; stir in green onions and next 3 ingredients. Cook 1 minute or until thoroughly heated. Stir in 3 tablespoons butter until melted. Yield: 12 servings.

editor's favorite • make ahead

Grits Dressing

This unique Southern dressing sports crusty grits croutons and spicy sausage. Serve it for Sunday brunch or Christmas dinner. Make the croutons and brown the sausage a day in advance.

Prep: 20 min. Cook: 1 hr., 20 min. Other: 20 min.

3   (10½-ounce) cans condensed chicken broth, undiluted
1¼ cups uncooked quick-cooking grits
1   cup freshly grated Parmesan cheese
1   pound ground hot pork sausage
⅓   cup butter or margarine
5   celery ribs with leaves, finely chopped
4   garlic cloves, minced (about 1 tablespoon)
1   large onion, chopped
1   large egg, lightly beaten
½   cup chopped fresh flat-leaf parsley

Bring broth to a boil in a large saucepan. Stir in grits, and return to a boil. Cover, reduce heat, and simmer 7 minutes or until grits are thickened, stirring twice. Stir in cheese. Remove from heat.

Great Cakes

*These are our staff's favorite
layer cakes for wowing family and friends
during the holidays.*

A whole lot of luscious layer cakes have come through our Test Kitchens over the past several decades. But these five are a stellar sampling of all that's good about dessert—moist layers, decadent frosting, impressive appearance, and most of all, delicious flavor. So in celebration of the 25th anniversary of *Christmas with Southern Living*®, let the baking begin.

Butter-Pecan Cake

Butter-Pecan Cake

The buttery goodness of white chocolate flavors this cake.

Prep: 20 min.   Cook: 22 min.   Other: 10 min.

Butter-Pecan Frosting
6   ounces white chocolate, chopped
½   cup boiling water
1   cup butter, softened
1½ cups sugar
4   large eggs, separated
1   teaspoon vanilla extract
1   cup buttermilk
1   teaspoon baking soda
3   cups sifted cake flour
Garnish: toasted pecan halves

Prepare frosting; cover and chill. Place white chocolate in a bowl. Pour boiling water over white chocolate; stir until smooth. Set aside, and let cool.

Grease 3 (9") round cakepans; line with wax paper. Grease and flour wax paper. Set aside.

Beat butter at medium speed with an electric mixer until creamy; gradually add sugar, beating well. Add egg yolks, 1 at a time, beating after each addition until blended. Stir in white chocolate and vanilla.

Combine buttermilk and soda. Add flour to butter mixture alternately with buttermilk mixture, beginning and ending with flour. Mix at low speed after each addition until blended.

Beat egg whites at high speed until stiff peaks form. Gently fold into batter. Pour batter into prepared pans.

Bake at 350° for 20 to 22 minutes or until a wooden pick inserted in center comes out clean. Cool in pans 10 minutes; remove from pans, and cool completely on wire racks.

Spread Butter-Pecan Frosting between layers and on top and sides of cake. Garnish, if desired. Store cake in refrigerator. Yield: 1 (3-layer) cake.

butter-pecan frosting

Prep: 7 min.   Cook: 11 min.   Other: 1 hr.

2   tablespoons butter
1¼ cups coarsely chopped pecans
1   (8-ounce) package cream cheese, softened
1   (3-ounce) package cream cheese, softened
½   cup butter, softened
1   (16-ounce) package powdered sugar
2   teaspoons vanilla extract

Melt 2 tablespoons butter in a large skillet over medium heat. Add pecans, and cook, stirring constantly, 10 minutes or until pecans are toasted. Remove from heat. Cool completely.

Beat cream cheese and ½ cup butter at medium speed with an electric mixer until creamy. Gradually add sugar; beat until light and fluffy. Stir in buttered pecans and vanilla. Cover and chill at least 1 hour. Yield: 4 cups.

Holiday Fig Cake

The presence of fresh rosemary is a highlight in this moist spice cake.

Prep: 40 min.   Cook: 45 min.   Other: 10 min.

1¾ cups fig preserves (almost 2 [11.5-ounce] jars)
3   large eggs
1   cup sugar
1   cup vegetable oil
2   cups all-purpose flour
1   teaspoon baking soda
1   teaspoon salt
1   teaspoon ground cinnamon
1   teaspoon ground allspice
½   teaspoon ground nutmeg
½   cup buttermilk
1   cup chopped pecans, toasted
1   cup finely chopped prunes
2   tablespoons chopped fresh rosemary (optional)
Honey-Cream Cheese Frosting
1¾ cups coarsely chopped pecans, toasted (optional)
Garnish: fresh rosemary sprigs

Chop large pieces of fig preserves, if necessary; set aside.

Beat eggs, sugar, and oil at medium speed with an electric mixer until blended. Combine flour and next 5 ingredients; add to sugar mixture alternately with buttermilk, beginning and ending with flour mixture. Fold in fig preserves, 1 cup chopped pecans, prunes, and, if desired, chopped rosemary.

Pour batter into 2 greased and floured 8" round cakepans. Bake at 350° for 42 to 45 minutes or until a wooden pick inserted in center comes out clean. Run a knife around edge of pans. Cool in pans on wire racks 10 minutes; remove from pans, and cool on wire racks.

Spread Honey-Cream Cheese Frosting between layers and on top and sides of cake. Press pecan pieces onto sides of cake, if desired. Garnish, if desired. Store cake in refrigerator. Yield: 1 (2-layer) cake.

honey-cream cheese frosting

Prep: 6 min.

1½ (8-ounce) packages cream cheese, softened
⅓   cup butter, softened
1½ tablespoons honey
4   cups powdered sugar

Beat cream cheese, butter, and honey at medium speed with an electric mixer just until smooth. Gradually add powdered sugar, beating at low speed just until blended. Yield: 3½ cups.

test kitchens 10 secrets to layer cake success

baking the layers

• Use shortening when a cake recipe calls for a "greased pan" unless otherwise specified.
• Don't sift flour before measuring, except for cake flour. Simply stir the flour, spoon it gently into a dry measuring cup, and level the top.
• Stagger cakepans on center rack of a preheated oven. If placed on separate racks, stagger pans so air can circulate.
• Keep oven door closed until minimum baking time has elapsed. Every time you open the oven door, the oven temperature drops 25 to 30 degrees. Use the oven window and light, instead, so you don't risk uneven baking.
• Keep several wire cooling racks on hand. Cakes that cool on a solid surface may become soggy.

assembling the cake

• Be sure cake layers are completely cooled before adding filling and frosting, or frosting may slide off the cake.
• Place bottom cake layer upside-down on the serving plate. Place top layer right side up.

frosting and freezing the cake

• Keep frosting just ahead of spatula. Do not backstroke until entire area is frosted, or spatula may drag crumbs into frosting.
• Frost sides of cake first, and top last.
• Unfrosted cake layers freeze best. Wrap cooled cake layers in aluminum foil, and then in plastic wrap. Freeze up to 5 months. Thaw cake layers in wrapping at room temperature.

Holiday Fig Cake

A rosemary wreath garnish hints at the unique use of herbs in this holiday cake.

Double-Nut Drenched Chocolate Cake

❄️ *editor's favorite*

Double-Nut Drenched Chocolate Cake

The layers of this decadent cake are drenched with Frangelico liqueur and then iced with fudgy topping.

Prep: 35 min. Cook: 21 min. Other: 10 min.

¾   cup butter, softened
2   cups firmly packed light brown sugar
2   large eggs
¾   cup water
¼   cup white vinegar
2   cups all-purpose flour
1   teaspoon baking soda
¼   teaspoon salt
1   cup finely chopped hazelnuts, toasted
1   tablespoon vanilla extract
¼   cup unsweetened cocoa
½   cup hazelnut liqueur (we tested with Frangelico)
Chocolate Topping
Garnish: hazelnuts

Grease 3 (8") round cakepans; line bottoms with wax paper. Grease and flour wax paper and sides of pans; set aside.

Beat butter at medium speed with an electric mixer until creamy; gradually add brown sugar, beating well. Add eggs, 1 at a time, beating until blended after each addition.

Combine water and vinegar. Combine flour, baking soda, and salt; add to butter mixture alternately with water mixture, beginning and ending with flour mixture. Beat at low speed until blended after each addition. Stir in chopped hazelnuts and vanilla. Pour one-third of batter into each of 2 prepared pans. Fold cocoa into remaining batter; pour chocolate batter into third pan.

Bake at 350° for 19 to 21 minutes or until a wooden pick inserted in center comes out clean. Cool in pans on wire racks 10 minutes; remove from pans. Peel off wax paper immediately after inverting. Cool completely on wire racks.

Brush liqueur over cake layers. Place 1 white cake layer, top side down, on serving plate; spread one-third of Chocolate Topping over top (do not frost sides). Top with chocolate cake layer; spread one-third Chocolate Topping over chocolate layer (do not frost sides). Top with remaining white layer and remaining Chocolate Topping (do not frost sides). Garnish, if desired. Allow cake to set several hours before slicing. Yield: 1 (3-layer) cake.

chocolate topping

Prep: 4 min. Cook: 9 min. Other: 55 min.

6   (4-ounce) sweet chocolate baking bars, chopped (we tested with Baker's German sweet chocolate)
1   pound butter
1½ cups chopped pecans
2   teaspoons vanilla extract

Melt chocolate and butter in a heavy saucepan over medium-low heat; cool 10 minutes. Stir in pecans and vanilla; cool mixture until spreading consistency, stirring occasionally (about 45 minutes). Yield: 5 cups.

Four ingredients become **sinfully** good frosting.

Hazel's Fresh Coconut Cake

Southerner Hazel Burwell has been making this stately cake for her family for over 40 years. She brushes the layers with a coconut syrup to keep the cake moist, and adds marshmallows to the frosting to keep it soft.

Prep: 1 hr., 15 min.   Cook: 20 min.   Other: 10 min.

1   cup butter, softened
2   cups sugar
4   large eggs
2¾ cups all-purpose flour
2   teaspoons baking powder
1   teaspoon salt
1   cup milk
1½ teaspoons vanilla extract
1½ teaspoons almond extract
2   tablespoons sugar
¼   cup fresh coconut milk
Boiled Frosting
2 to 3 cups fresh shredded coconut
      (about 2 coconuts)
Garnishes: kumquats, crab apples

Beat butter at medium speed with an electric mixer until creamy; gradually add 2 cups sugar, beating well. Add eggs, 1 at a time, beating until blended after each addition.

Combine flour, baking powder, and salt; add to butter mixture alternately with milk, beginning and ending with flour mixture. Beat at low speed until blended after each addition. Stir in flavorings. Pour batter into 3 greased and floured 9" round cakepans.

choosing coconuts

When choosing a coconut, carefully examine the eyes at the base of the coconut. Check this area for any signs of mold or mildew. Shake several good candidates to determine which one has the most milk. Your goal is a dry, solid coconut, heavy for its size, with plenty of milk.

Bake at 350° for 18 to 20 minutes or until a wooden pick inserted in center comes out clean. Cool in pans on wire racks 10 minutes; remove from pans, and cool on wire racks.

Combine 2 tablespoons sugar and coconut milk in a small glass bowl. Microwave on HIGH 1 minute; stir until sugar dissolves. Brush 1 cake layer with half of coconut milk mixture, leaving a ½" margin around edges. Spread with 1 cup Boiled Frosting, and sprinkle with ½ cup shredded coconut. Top with second cake layer, and repeat procedure. Top with remaining cake layer. Spread remaining frosting on top and sides of cake; sprinkle with remaining coconut. Garnish, if desired. Yield: 1 (3-layer) cake.

Fresh coconut cake is the essence of Christmas.

Hazel's Fresh Coconut Cake

boiled frosting

Prep: 9 min.   Cook: 10 min.

1½   cups sugar
½   cup water
4   egg whites
½   teaspoon cream of tartar
⅛   teaspoon salt
6   large marshmallows, cut into small pieces

Combine sugar and water in a heavy saucepan. Cook over medium heat, stirring constantly, until mixture is clear. Cook, without stirring, until syrup reaches soft ball stage or candy thermometer registers 240° (about 10 minutes).

While syrup cooks, beat egg whites at low speed with an electric mixer until foamy. Add cream of tartar and salt; beat at medium speed until soft peaks form. Increase to high speed, and add hot syrup in a heavy stream. Add marshmallows, a few pieces at a time. Beat until stiff peaks form and frosting is thick enough to spread. Yield: 7¼ cups.

*New Orleans Double-Chocolate
Praline-Fudge Cake*

New Orleans Double-Chocolate Praline-Fudge Cake

This cake is off-the-charts rich. If you like pralines, you'll love this candylike frosting.

Prep: 50 min.   Cook: 29 min.   Other: 55 min.

1   cup butter or margarine
¼   cup unsweetened cocoa
1   cup water
½   cup buttermilk
2   large eggs
1   teaspoon baking soda
1   teaspoon vanilla extract
2   cups sugar
2   cups all-purpose flour
½   teaspoon salt
Chocolate Ganache
Praline Frosting

Grease bottoms of 3 (8") round cakepans; line with wax paper. Grease and flour wax paper and sides of pans.

Cook first 3 ingredients in a saucepan over low heat, stirring constantly, until butter melts and mixture is smooth; remove from heat. Cool.

Beat buttermilk, eggs, baking soda, and vanilla at medium speed with an electric mixer until smooth. Add butter mixture to buttermilk mixture, beating until blended. Combine sugar, flour, and salt; gradually add to buttermilk mixture, beating until blended. (Batter will be thin.) Pour batter evenly into prepared pans.

Bake at 350° for 20 to 22 minutes or until a wooden pick inserted in center comes out clean. Cool in pans on wire racks 10 minutes. Remove from pans; immediately remove wax paper. Cool completely on wire racks. (Layers will appear thin.)

Spread about ½ cup ganache between cake layers; spread remainder on sides of cake (do not frost top of cake). Chill cake 30 minutes. Pour Praline Frosting slowly over top of cake, spreading to edges, and allowing some frosting to run over sides of cake. Freeze, if desired; thaw at room temperature 4 to 6 hours. Yield: 1 (3-layer) cake.

chocolate ganache

Cook: 3 min.   Other: 25 min.

2   cups (12 ounces) semisweet chocolate morsels
⅓   cup whipping cream
¼   cup butter or margarine, cut into pieces

Microwave chocolate morsels and cream in a glass bowl on MEDIUM (50% power) 2 to 3 minutes or until morsels are melted, stirring after 1½ minutes; whisk until smooth. Gradually add butter, whisking until smooth. Cool, whisking often, about 25 minutes or until spreading consistency. Yield: about 2 cups.

praline frosting

Don't prepare this candylike frosting ahead because it'll harden very quickly.

Cook: 4 min.   Other: 5 min.

¼   cup butter or margarine
1   cup firmly packed light brown sugar
⅓   cup whipping cream
1   cup powdered sugar
1   teaspoon vanilla extract
1   cup chopped pecans, toasted

Bring first 3 ingredients to a boil in a 2-quart saucepan over medium heat, stirring often; boil 1 minute. Remove from heat, and whisk in powdered sugar and vanilla until smooth. Add toasted pecans, stirring gently 3 to 5 minutes or until frosting begins to cool and thicken slightly. Pour frosting immediately over cake. Yield: about 2 cups.

25 Classic Wreaths

From a simple evergreen to a circle of chocolates, the wreath is the quintessential holiday trim. On these pages we share our favorites from the last 25 years.

◄ Holly and Pine

Express the essence of the season with a red-and-green
wreath—perhaps the most traditional composition of all.

▲ Merry Bells

Hang small wreaths from ribbons accented with bells.
Every time the door is opened, you'll enjoy a cheery hello.

tried & true tips for making wreaths

Hanging a wreath on the front door signals the start of the Christmas season and extends a warm welcome. Here are some tools that make wreath making easy.

base basics

Florist foam. Soak this wreath form in water, and let it drain before adding decorations. It's the best choice for keeping such materials as greenery and flowers fresh. Mist with water every few days for maximum freshness.

Plastic craft foam and straw. Perhaps the easiest forms to embellish, use these for wreath decorations that don't need to be keep moist, such as magnolia leaves, moss, ornaments, and pinecones.

Grapevine. This base doesn't have to be covered entirely, so you may need fewer materials to finish the wreath. Grapevine wreaths are especially good for wiring on decorations, such as ornaments and holiday trinkets. For greenery and berries, just tuck the stems between the branches of the wreath.

strong attachments

Florist wire. Whether on a spool or in single pieces, florist wire is an essential tool for decorating a wreath. Use it to attach ornaments, greenery sprigs, berries, pinecones, and ribbons. It's very flexible and easy to use.

Florist picks. Use picks to attach fruits to wreaths. Picks are available either plain or with wire attached to one end. If decorating a grapevine wreath, for example, use picks with wire so that you can stick the sharp end of a pick into each fruit and use the wire end to attach it to the wreath.

Florist pins. U-shaped florist pins hold leaves, greenery and berry stems, and moss securely in place on straw and plastic craft-foam wreaths. These pins can be removed easily and used again.

Hot-glue gun. Use a hot-glue gun to permanently attach such items as ornaments, pinecones, moss, and ribbons to a wreath you plan to use again next year.

where to find it

Look for all the materials mentioned at crafts and discount centers.

Fraser Fir and Flowers
Update a standard greenery wreath with chartreuse 'Kermit' mums and bronze ribbon.

▲ Feathers and Magnolia
Fashion a splendid circle of pine, magnolia, and cypress. Crown it with feathers and faux apples.

▲ Ornaments Abound
Hot-glue bright ornaments in varying sizes to a straw wreath for a fun decoration that will last for years.

▲ Aucuba and Nandina
Add pizzazz to an evergreen wreath by wiring on aucuba leaves, nandina berries, and lotus pods.

▼ Carnation Ring
Snuggle together bright red carnations on a florist-foam wreath for a fresh twist on tradition.

▼ Garden Inspired
Adorn a wreath with wild abandon. Give plum branches, cedar, dried hydrangea, and beautyberries a try.

▼ Winter White
Think of red birds in the snow when you pair red ribbon and berries with baby's breath and paperwhites.

◀ Stocking Stuffer

Start with a twiggy wreath. Then lavish it with magnolia leaves, holly, seeded eucalyptus, and red and white gerbera daisies. Complete the look with a jaunty bow and a velvet stocking for a touch of whimsy.

Southwestern Flavor ▼

For regional flair, include dried peppers along with traditional adornments on a grapevine wreath. Enhance the theme with a burlap bow, dried grasses, and feathers.

▲ Williamsburg Classic

Evoke Colonial times with an evergreen wreath adorned with fresh fruits, including that Southern symbol of hospitality: the pineapple.

Vine-Wreath Snowman

Build the perfect Southern snowman with three grapevine wreaths, a stovepipe hat, a scarf, and boots. To make the hat, shape sheet metal and spray-paint it black; or affix a large coffee can to a semicircle of wood, and paint it black.

Herbs and Toile

Wrap a straw or plastic craft-foam wreath form with strips of toile fabric. Wire on clay pots filled with herbs and berries. Accent with gingham fabric.

▲ Sand Dollar Adornments

Garnish an evergreen wreath with creamy white sand dollars for a seaside theme.

▲ New Heights

Suspend a double-sided wreath (greenery on both sides) with ribbons above a table for a fresh approach.

▲ Market Fresh

Check out the produce aisle to trim a festive kitchen wreath with vegetables and gerbera daisies. Finish the look with a gingham bow.

▼ Family Treasures

Fill a wreath with favorite collectibles, and bring back fond memories season after season.

▼ Chocolate Treat

For a sweet decoration, use a low-temp glue gun to secure candies and a bow to a grapevine wreath.

▼ Simple Statement

Use a ribbon hanger as the only embellishment for a wreath made by pinning leaves to a plastic form.

▲ Apples and Holly

Tuck small lady apples, sprigs of holly, and greenery clippings among the branches of a grapevine wreath for a casual look with lots of charm.

▲ Berry Blend

Cover a small grapevine wreath with pepperberries and holly berries. Stick the sturdy holly stems between the vines; wire the pepperberries in place with florist wire.

▲ Golden Fruits and Berries

Use permanent materials for a wreath that makes return showings for years to come. Wire together pears, apples, pomegranates, and berries; then shape the garland into a rectangle.

▼ Urn of Plenty

For a tabletop showpiece, stand a vine wreath laced with holly-berry stems in an urn mounded with flowers and fruits. Secure pieces in florist foam with florist picks.

▲ Natural Selection

Hot-glue nuts, pinecones, and star anise to a grapevine wreath. Sprigs of pine provide a woodsy accent and fresh Christmassy scent.

Joyful Decorations

Get ready to deck the halls, doors, and windows
with dozens of delightful trims that will make your
home sparkle with holiday merriment.

Ways to Say Welcome

*Give holiday guests a cheerful greeting
with festive outdoor designs.*

Extend a Warm Reception

Use lively colors, such as the red and chartreuse ribbons on these "presents" (actually
empty boxes), to add surefire impact to your front porch decorations. The door is
accented with a wreath and metal bucket attached with florist wire. Flowers and
greenery tucked in the bucket stay fresh for several days in moistened florist foam.
Adding the bucket is a clever way to update the traditional wreath.

◄ Add Accents in Unexpected Places

Try a shutter instead of a window as the backdrop for natural decorations. Fill a wire wall basket with greenery and berries, and wire it in place. This is one of the easiest decorations to make: The clippings practically arrange themselves, and they'll stay fresh for several days even without florist foam. Pinecones hide the stems and help hold them in place.

▼ Go Natural

Simple touches often convey the warmest greetings. For this quaint embellishment, wire together oversize pinecones and loop them over a lantern. Tuck greenery boughs behind the pinecones for a rich contrast. If you don't have large pinecones, wire together several small ones to achieve a similar effect.

tools for natural decorations

Gather key items before you start decorating so that you can concentrate your creative energy and make the whole process more fun. Here are some suggestions:

- Pair of sharp clippers
- Bucket of water to hold greenery clippings
- Assorted vases and containers
- Florist foam, florist wire, and florist picks
- Wired ribbon

◀ Spell Out a Sentiment

Send a seasonal greeting by shaping letters from plastic craft foam and covering them with sprigs of boxwood or mixed greenery. In cool weather the greenery looks fresh up to two weeks. For a permanent version, use faux greenery. These evergreen letters work well indoors hanging in a window or propped on a mantel.

▼ Make Your Own Reindeer Family

Cut wood sections from a small tree trunk or branch for the bodies, heads, necks, and legs; use twiggy branches for the antlers and magnolia leaves for the ears and tails. Drill holes to assemble the pieces; if desired, glue to secure. Add bows to dress them for the holidays.

Dress a Tray for Instant Charm

An ironwork tray—or most any circular metal piece—is a quick starting point for a wreath. Use florist wire to attach bunches of berries or greenery to the sides of the piece. Hang the tray on a door or wall for an easy holiday accent. If you like, wire an ornament or bow to the bottom of the wreath.

A Jolly Topiary

*This decoration is so much fun to make that you'll want to include the whole family. It's merely
a matter of stacking wreaths, starting with the largest and ending with the smallest.*

Place a circle of plywood or particleboard on top of a container to make a secure base for the tree (Photo 1).

To build the topiary, stack embellished wreath forms (see next paragraph) in incrementally smaller diameters in the following order: a moistened florist-foam ring (for greenery), an unadorned grapevine wreath, and then a craft plastic ring (for apples; see Photo 2). Continue in this order to finish the tree. Top with apples held together with a florist pick; tuck a few sprigs of greenery around the apples.

To embellish the wreaths, stick sprigs of greenery around the edges of the florist-foam rings. For the apple rings, wrap the wreath forms with sheet moss to hide the forms; use florist picks to attach the apples (Photo 2).

A Spirited Mix

Let these ideas inspire you to dress your home with a beautiful blend of seasonal trends and traditions.

▲ Enhance the Enchantment

With all the beautiful plants available at Christmas, it's tempting to let individual pots stand alone. But if you want a more dynamic decoration, gather the pots into one large container for an engaging focal point that will last throughout the holidays. Here, pots of amaryllis, poinsettia, and maidenhair fern converge in a copper container and blend harmoniously with the painting for even more impact. If needed, use moss to conceal the tops of the individual pots.

◄ Create a Scheme

Luscious browns and deep reds convey a cozy charm at every turn in this inviting family room. To hang fruit from a chandelier, tie ribbons to stems; or use florist picks with wires to attach the fruit to the ribbons. To make the centerpiece, use florist picks to attach pears to a florist-foam or plastic craft-foam tree. Stick pepperberries between the pears to fill in gaps.

Buy multiples of festive metal cones.
They're among the most versatile items to have on hand for the holidays.

◄ Make a Cake That's a Lasting Treat

This floral cake is a delightful centerpiece that gets rave reviews. Cover the sides and top edges of a block of moistened florist foam with tiny mums. (These chartreuse beauties are 'Kermit' mums. Use larger blooms, such as carnations, for a less expensive version.) For the topper, stick stems of flowers, greenery, and berries into the foam and add ribbons. Place the foam on a plate or on plastic to protect surfaces. The arrangement should stay fresh about one week.

Go Up and Over the Top

This window treatment goes all out, and its placement in a high-profile location makes the effort pay off in a big way. This is a good approach if you want to concentrate your decorations for maximum impact. The greenery stays fresh for a week to 10 days.

For a special gathering, fresh flowers take an evergreen garland to the next level. Here, blocks of florist foam are secured at the corners of the garland and filled with fresh blooms and greenery. Flowers in water vials are tucked along the garland and in the wreath. Look for roses at grocery stores and discount centers, or substitute less expensive blooms for a similar look.

Explore Alternatives

This luxuriously adorned stairway and mantel prove that there's more than one festive color combination for holiday decorations. Regal blue and sumptuous brown ribbons are complemented by bronze, gold, and blue ornaments. A mix of greenery—fir, pine, cedar, and magnolia—in the garland and on the mantel creates a lively blend of textures.

For the garland, wire together several small branches; then wire together the small bundles to form a garland. Use fabric-wrapped florist wire or chenille stems to avoid making scratches on the wooden railing. For the mantel, layer branches and tuck in small pieces of greenery to achieve the desired look; wire the ornaments in place.

Backyard and woods clippings are excellent sources for fresh materials for holiday decorating. Also look for greenery bundles at home-improvement stores, or ask for the leftover trimmings at a Christmas tree lot. For long-lasting freshness, place the greenery in a bucket of water overnight before using it in decorations.

Grace your table or buffet with tree-shaped topiaries. Moist florist-foam bases keep them fresh all season long.

Double the Elegance

For a frosty shimmer, take advantage of mirrors to multiply the effect of glistening glass. The brightly wrapped gift, lush flowers in the angel wall vases, and moss-covered balls and rosebuds in the tureen add a colorful complement to the crystal lamps and finials.

Play a Theme

For all its grandeur, this look is simple to arrange using items you already have. Red
flowers and berries are a vibrant counterpoint to the groupings of silver serving pieces.
Bits of greenery tucked along the shelves bring the separate elements together for a
well-planned look.

Favorite collectibles make dynamic **seasonal arrangements.**
Accent them with **flowers or candies** in holiday colors for **easy decorations.**

Wrap Up an Elegant Look

Silk and velvet ribbons turn a plastic wreath form into a thing of beauty. The ribbons—which are wrapped around the wreath and held in place with straight pins—can be unwrapped and used again after the holidays. A colorful mix of ribbons tied to the wreath hangs it where desired. Fanciful ornaments and oodles of bows add to the abundant look.

Christmas Cottage Charm

Feel the magic of the season in a cozy home that overflows with holiday delights.

Conjure a Holiday Fairyland

The enchantment begins at the front door of this charming abode (above) that opens onto a roomy screened porch that's decked from floor to ceiling with Christmas cheer (right). The traditional red-and-white theme is updated with generous doses of natural colors and materials, as seen in the linen pillows, pinecone garlands, ornaments, gift wrappings, and chocolate brown dinner plates.

get the cottage look

Gather your favorite decorations and then add some new ones for a beautifully coordinated Christmas setting.

start with a plan

• Decide on the main colors you want to use. You may want to stay with red and green but accent with another color, as with the brown accessories used for this home.
• Think about all the areas and ways you want to decorate, including centerpieces and other table decorations that you want.
• Make a list of the decorations you need to replace and the new things you want to add.

consider flowers and greenery

• Outdoor garlands and wreaths stay fresh longer than the same greenery indoors due to cooler outdoor temperatures. Misting the greenery helps keep it fresh. Plan on greenery staying fresh for a week to 10 days indoors and up to a couple of weeks outdoors.
• Arrange flowers just before a special party for maximum freshness. Or use such flowering plants as paperwhites, poinsettias, cyclamen, and amaryllis that last throughout the season and beyond.

accessorize

• Browse cabinets and cupboards for everyday items that carry out your decorating scheme.
• Incorporate natural materials for a cozy ambience.

all in the details

Wrap gift packages with papers and ribbons that blend with other decorations. Tie ribbons in fluffy bows for a homey touch. ▼

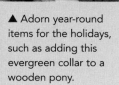

▲ Tie felt ornaments to the tree to add a handcrafted touch.
◀ Incorporate angels or other symbols of the season in outdoor containers for quick holiday embellishments.

▲ Adorn year-round items for the holidays, such as adding this evergreen collar to a wooden pony.

◀ Plan a Centerpiece with Staying Power

Topiaries—found easily during the Christmas season at grocery stores and home-improvement centers—can be the basis for a tabletop decoration that lasts for weeks. This topiary is encircled with pears and accented with berries. Use florist picks to hold the fruit in place.

▲ Keep It Simple

A pot of paperwhites, ruffly white anemones, and a scattering of fruits and greenery twigs are easy to assemble for a mantel decoration with loads of charm. Solid white pitchers and a red flowerpot allow the smaller elements to stand out.

▲ Do the Unexpected

Use Christmas stockings to add a holiday note all through the house. Even on a dining room hutch, a soft velvet stocking seems right at home and is a fitting complement to the seasonal display.

◀ Form a Group

Arrange several small items together for a big decorative impact. Here, the wreath and the pine sprigs that are sprinkled among the pieces provide a pleasing framework for the trees, reindeer, candles, and pitcher.

Holiday Style Secrets

Our photo stylists give tips on making the most of your decorating efforts.

Make a Big Impression

As a photo stylist, Amy Wilson (above) arranges things for a living. When it comes to Christmas, she believes in concentrating on key areas, such as the mantel (right). Large vases, holding spray-painted red twigs, anchor the mantel arrangement. Tall wooden vases add height, and two small red vases contain loosely arranged tulips for a fun sense of movement and energy. The red lampshade, pillows, and tray enliven the scheme.

Focus on a central area to showcase your favorite decorations for a dynamic presentation.—Amy Wilson

get the look

Amy suggests painting canvases and hanging them above the mantel (below), whether for Christmas or year-round. She selected the Christmas decorations to complement the shades of red found in these canvases.

start with a plan

• Establish a focal point. Amy spread drywall mud on 12 (8- x 10-inch) canvases to create a rough texture. After the mud dried, she painted the canvases with varying shades of red latex wall paint. Hung with tiny nails above the mantel, the canvases become the center of attention and establish the color palette for the room's decorations.
• Mix in a few neutral elements to balance the main colors. Amy used wooden vases to offer a pleasing contrast with the dark red containers (left).

consider flowers and greenery

• Tuck sprigs of greenery and berries among separate items in an arrangement to unify the appearance.
• Include flowers for a fresh accent. Here, tulips contribute a contemporary note (left and below).

accessorize

• Use ornaments as decorative elements. Placed among the greenery, ornaments in various sizes add color and twinkles of light (left).
• Rely on votive candles to contribute a festive glow.

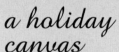

a holiday canvas

▲ Think of household items in new ways. This tiny cranberry-colored wreath is actually a napkin ring.
◀ Tie petite vases to garland, and fill them with small blooms.

Add small details, such as these candles and
tiny vases, to express your personal style.

Play Out a Theme

"A good way to plan your holiday decorations is to find one idea that will set your scheme in motion," says stylist Kay Clarke. For her, dining room chairs proved to be just the inspiration. The deep red, green, and ivory stripes on the chairs suggested a color combination that Kay was able to use throughout the room. For the dinnerware, she mixed and matched colors. Kay then repeated the scheme with red flowers in the centerpiece and ivory ornament favors tied with green ribbons. For a finishing touch, Kay featured striped candy canes in glasses and candy wreaths hung from the chandelier and used as napkin rings.

My favorite holiday decorating ideas involve the whole family. —Kay Clarke

Let Treats Do Double Duty

Kay and her family celebrate the season by baking goodies together, and she gives the results center stage on the dining room sideboard. Kay also fills glass jars and cake stands with cookies and candies for a sumptuous arrangement. Hard candies and jelly beans add sparks of color.

sweet accents

▲ Include the family to make holiday decorating more special. Kay's daughters, Melanie and Julie, helped style the table.▼

▲ Add playful elements to the setting, like these candy canes in glasses.
◄ Tie candy wreaths (or ornaments) to the chandelier for a fanciful focal point.

get the look

Decide on the areas you want to dress for the holidays.
Then involve the whole family to create a cozy look
and heartwarming memories.

start with a plan

• Let your home's furnishings suggest a color theme. Or
go all out with traditional reds, greens, silvers, and golds.
• Reinforce your color scheme with such decorative
elements as ornaments, ribbons, candies, and flowers.
• Introduce color in unexpected places, such as red
candies in a candleholder (right).

consider flowers and greenery

• If you use a clear vase for cut flowers, angle the stems
for a more attractive display. Then trim the stems ends
and change the water every few days to keep the
arrangement looking fresh (left).
• String garlands in unexpected places, such as around
mirrors (left).

accessorize

• Use cake stands and clear glass containers for festive
displays. Food treats, ornaments, nuts, pinecones, and
citrus fruits are just a few good fillers (below).
• Mix and match dinnerware to add interest to the
table setting.

◄ Kay's grandsons, Banton and Sterling,
decorate a white cake with star-shaped
cookies they baked. The stars on the
sides of the cake are held in place with
canned decorator frosting. ▼

Nuts About Christmas

*Make this seasonal treat the main ingredient
in fun and fanciful decorations.*

▲ Add Natural Elegance

This dining table decoration is as simple to create as it
looks: Place votive holders in a curving line in the center
of the table. Tuck in sprigs of greenery; then scatter an
assortment of nuts along the arrangement.

Fill in the Spaces ▶

Use a variety of nuts to enhance a tabletop arrangement.
Here, walnuts, almonds, chestnuts, and pecans fall easily
into the gaps between the fruits that cover the base of
the ivy ring.

◀ Go for Glamour

Rosy red lilies and seeded eucalyptus are high-style additions to a wire stocking stuffed with nuts. When using nuts in your holiday decorations, consider the colors of the shells. Here, light and dark shades offer a pleasing contrast. Place flower stems in water vials to keep them fresh.

▲ Glue On Accents

Nuts and white tallow berries are elegant embellishments on a square boxwood-and-eucalyptus wreath. Use a hot-glue gun to attach the nuts and florist wire to secure the berries and bow.

keeping nuts fresh

• Because nuts contain high amounts of oil, they can go rancid and develop a stale taste fairly quickly. Nuts in the shell keep well for six months to a year if stored in a cool, dark, dry place.

• Store shelled nuts in airtight containers. They'll stay fresh at room temperature up to a month or if refrigerated from three to six months.

• Freeze nuts in zip-top freezer bags up to a year. Store vacuum-packed nuts at room temperature.

• Nuts that have been painted should not be eaten.

▲ Pair Bold Colors

Dress up nuts with metallic-hued rub-on color (we used Rub 'n Buff). The silver-toned nuts and rich red pears and candles combine for a spirited presentation that's surprisingly simple.

Include Nuts on the Buffet ▶

Large clear vases filled with an abundance of nuts and long branches of pyracantha are eye-catching showpieces. Since these nuts are still in their shells, they can be used for cooking and eating after the tableau is disassembled. To minimize the number of nuts needed, place a block of florist foam or other filler in the center of each vase and fill in with nuts.

◀ Go All Out

Nuts are fitting additions to a display of collectible
nutcrackers, putting them readily at hand for cracking
and eating. When arranging collections, elevate a few
of the pieces on boxes or upside-down bowls to create
a more intriguing composition.

▲ Treat Your Guests

Place paper cones stuffed with seasoned nuts in a fanciful
box filled with sugar or sand. Locate the box on a table
near the door so that holiday visitors can leave with
yummy parting gifts.

Make the Season Bright

Create a festive twinkle with shining ideas that feature candles.

▲ Send a Message

Handwrite or print out a seasonal sentiment on paper to adorn candleholders. For best results use vellum, a heavy translucent paper. Trim the vellum to cover the side of each large votive holder or small drinking glass. Wrap the vellum around the outside of each holder and use double-sided tape to hold the vellum in place. (Holders with straight sides are the easiest to wrap.) Place a tea light inside each holder.

Cast a Cheery Glow ▶

A showy cavalcade of candles is even more impressive when placed atop a mirror. Rose hips, pinecones, and greenery unite the individual pillars. The rosemary topiary adds height and provides a central focus.

◀ Soften the Edges

A rustic iron candelabra is transformed into a handsome centerpiece when embellished with bright red candles and a ring of evergreen clippings and variegated holly. Such iconic materials as holly, evergreens, and (especially red) candles instantly set a holiday mood.

▲ Make It Personal

Personalized candles are great gifts for family and friends. Handwrite or use a computer to create personalized labels on heavy-stock paper. Glue each label onto contrasting paper to create a framelike effect. Glue a band of ribbon around each candle; then glue the desired label onto the ribbon, covering the overlapped edges.

◀ Tie on a Trim

Add festivity to a candle grouping by encircling glass vases with ribbons. Use a dot of glue or double-sided tape to hold the ribbons in place. For the most appealing results, mix sheer and opaque ribbons.

Light the Way

These wire luminarias add candlelight in an outdoor setting, which is a welcoming treat for Christmas guests. Placing the garland along the stairs instead of on the railing provides a pretty backdrop for the candles.

Simple Expressions

These arrangements are quick, easy, and loaded with charm.

Stack Up Style

Nestle votive candles amidst red candies in clear holders, and then stack the holders for a look with lots of appeal. Fill the top container with flowers and greenery. Don't place a votive holder directly above a flame, and be sure to keep flames well above the candies.

Let It Snow

This stylish setting features Christmas red ribbons tied around red pillar candles. Silvery candleholders and tall glasses filled with small silver ornaments are a sparkling complement. A red ornament personalized with a silver pen marks each place. A sprinkling of faux snow heightens the holiday attitude.

Pinecones, apples, and acorns mirror the china for a coordinated centerpiece. Greenery tied with golden ribbon becomes an elegant chair decoration.

▲ Say It with Berries

Make a bold decorating statement in a hurry with berry stems, such as these deciduous holly berries. Sprigs of pine tucked among the stems hold the berries in place in a stately urn. Surrounding the scene with candles in the same deep hue as the berries and urn creates a dynamic arrangement. The ornaments reflect the candlelight, adding a warm sparkle.

◄ Set the Stage

Pair small decorative pieces to produce a more impressive display. Books tied with a bow and a small nativity scene are perfect partners when placed side by side.

Wrap Up a Design

Don't underestimate the power of wrapped packages to add a fun dimension to holiday arrangements. For this look, place a potted amaryllis in an urn and surround the plant with gaily wrapped boxes. Tuck greenery underneath the boxes to hide the pot.

Kick It Up a Notch

Layer on the charm, and take the standard stairway garland with bows to new heights.
Here, candy canes, a popcorn-and-cranberry garland, and sweet treats add a little magic
to this traditional decoration.

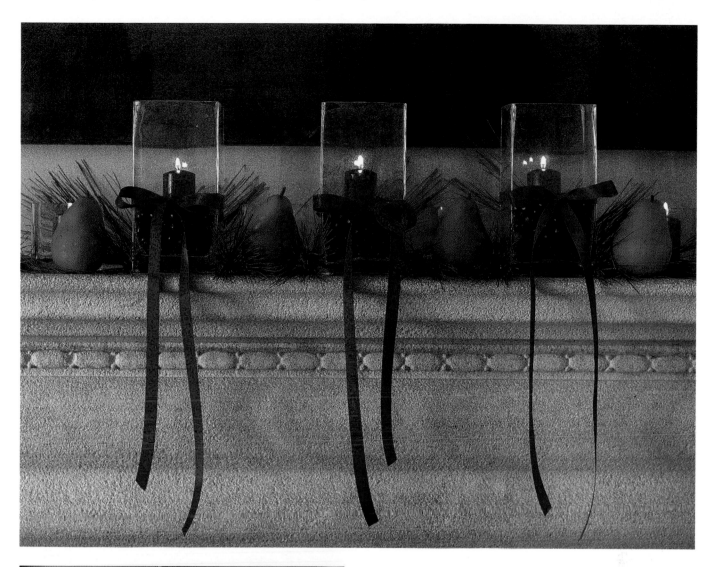

▲ Make It Easy on Yourself

This effortless design couldn't be more beautiful or serene. To get the look, fill one-third of each square vase with cranberries, place votives on top of the cranberries, and then tie a ribbon around each vase. Fill in between the vases with pears and pine sprigs. To enhance the glow, place short votive holders with candles behind the pears.

◀ Capitalize on Charm

Allow accessories to be a part of your holiday decorating. This extraordinary piece magnifies the impact of a wall vase filled with fresh blooms and hung in front of the mirror. Incorporating everyday items as a part of seasonal embellishments makes it easy to give every room a touch of Christmas.

Card Tricks

*Display your holiday greetings
with decorative flair.*

▲ Wire a Greeting

Bend flexible solder wire to shape card holders or a word. To make this arrangement, cover a florist-foam base with greenery clippings, berries, and flowers. Leave "stems" on the wire pieces to anchor them in the florist foam.

Decorate the Decoration ▶

An openwork iron piece offers a clever setting for showing off holiday cards. As cards arrive, punch holes in them and tie them to the piece. It provides a grand way to be reminded daily of warm wishes from family and friends.

▲ Clip on Cheer

Use paper or binder clips to attach Christmas cards to an unadorned wreath. By the end of the season, you'll have a display that's overflowing with good wishes.

Check Your Messages ▶

Paint a sheet of corkboard with a smart checkerboard design and place it in a fancy frame for a message center that spreads the news long after the holidays. Red thumbtacks hold items in place. (Find corkboard sheets at crafts stores and home-improvement centers.)

Hang On to Good Wishes

A trio of stylish trees adorned with candy canes and ornaments takes on special meaning when heartfelt greetings hang from the "branches." Punch holes in cards and party invitations, and tie them on with sheer ribbons.

Countdown to Christmas Dinner

'Tis the season for family gatherings and good food. The plan on these pages will help you produce a dynamite-tasting meal with time to spare. Take our make-ahead tips and prepare the whole menu, or just pick a recipe or two to add to your traditional meal.

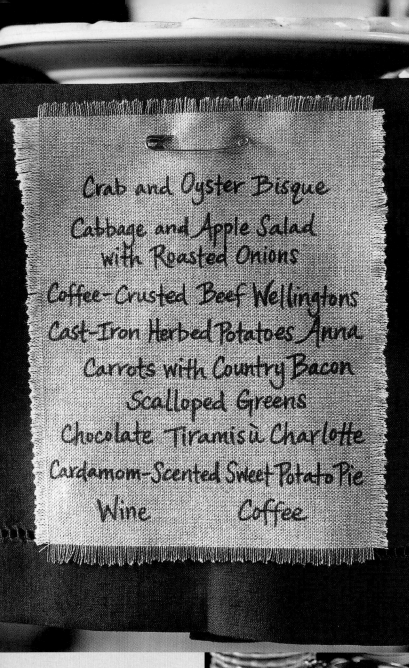

Crab and Oyster Bisque

Cabbage and Apple Salad
with Roasted Onions

Coffee-Crusted Beef Wellingtons

Cast-Iron Herbed Potatoes Anna

Carrots with Country Bacon

Scalloped Greens

Chocolate Tiramisù Charlotte

Cardamom-Scented Sweet Potato Pie

Wine   Coffee

menu for 8

the countdown

It's the biggest holiday celebration of the year. Let our timeline help you organize your meal preparation.

1 week to 1 month ahead:

- Make grocery list. Shop for nonperishables.
- Visit wine shop to select wines.
- Prepare Coffee-Crusted Beef Wellingtons; freeze.
- Plan centerpiece and other table decorations.

2 or 3 days ahead:

- Take inventory of china, serving dishes, and utensils. Gather whatever pieces you'll need. Polish silver.

1 day ahead:

- Prepare Chocolate Tiramisù Charlotte; refrigerate overnight.
- Blanch and peel pearl onions, and prepare dressing for salad; refrigerate overnight.
- Peel and slice carrots; refrigerate overnight.
- Prepare Scalloped Greens without breadcrumb topping, and refrigerate unbaked overnight.
- Set the table, complete with centerpiece.

morning of the meal:

- Prepare and bake Cardamom-Scented Sweet Potato Pie.

grace notes

▲ Label bowls and platters for specific recipes.
◄ Gather flatware and serving pieces.

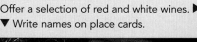

Offer a selection of red and white wines. ►
▼ Write names on place cards.

3 hours before the meal:

• Prepare and bake Cast-Iron Herbed Potatoes Anna.

2 hours before the meal:

• Add breadcrumb topping to Scalloped Greens, and bake; cover with foil to keep warm.
• Prepare Cabbage and Apple Salad with Roasted Onions.
• Prepare Carrots with Country Bacon.

45 minutes before the meal:

• Prepare Crab and Oyster Bisque; keep warm over low heat.
• Bake beef Wellingtons (do not thaw); finish sauce, and keep warm over low heat.

just before serving:

• Reheat side dishes in the oven and on stovetop as needed.
• Garnish beef Wellingtons with herbs.

just after dinner:

• Brew coffee.
• Set out desserts for guests to sample.

Garnish each entrée simply with fresh herbs.▼

▲ Toast dinner guests with a blessing. Serve coffee. It never fails with rich desserts. ►

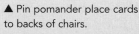

▲ Pin pomander place cards to backs of chairs.

get the look

For the special touches of Christmastime, find our best ideas this season below.

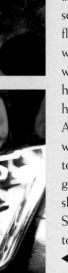

◀Decorate with versatile fir pomanders. Use them as part of a centerpiece or suspend them on chair backs as place card holders. To make pomanders, wrap Christmas tree clippings around 4" plastic craft foam balls, securing them with U-shape florist pins. For centerpiece, wrap each ball in ribbon and tie with a bow. For place card holders, thread ribbon through hole-punched place cards. Attach ribbon to pomanders with florist pins. Attach ribbon to chairs with straight pins. If greenery is fresh, pomanders should last up to 2 weeks. Spritz pomanders occasionally to refresh greenery.

◀Scout out antique or just unique salt and pepper cellars for each place setting.

◀Present a menu handwritten on fabric at each place setting. Use pinking shears from a craft store to cut out linen fabric swatches; fray edges, if desired. Write the menu on each fabric cutout, using a fabric pen. Attach the fabric swatch to the napkin at each place setting, using a large safety pin. (Alternatively, you can *print* your menu on fabric using a home computer. Computer Printer Fabric™ feeds directly into your printer. All you do is input your menu and pick a font that suits your holiday style.)

Crab and Oyster Bisque

This rich seafood soup earned our Test Kitchens highest rating.

Prep: 15 min.   Cook: 20 min.

¼ cup butter or margarine
4 garlic cloves, minced
2 shallots, finely chopped
3 tablespoons all-purpose flour
1 (8-ounce) bottle clam juice
1 cup dry white wine
1 tablespoon Worcestershire sauce
1 teaspoon Cajun seasoning
¼ teaspoon pepper
1 quart whipping cream
1 (12-ounce) container fresh oysters, drained
1 pound fresh lump crabmeat

Melt butter in a Dutch oven over medium heat; add garlic and shallot, and sauté until tender. Add flour; cook 1 minute, stirring constantly. Add clam juice and wine; cook 2 minutes or until thickened, stirring constantly.

Stir in Worcestershire sauce and next 3 ingredients. Cook until thoroughly heated, about 10 minutes. Stir in oysters and crabmeat; cook just until edges of oysters curl. Yield: 10 cups.

Serve crab and oyster bisque in little cups at the start of your meal.

Cabbage and Apple Salad with Roasted Onions

Cabbage and Apple Salad with Roasted Onions

It's worth the time to blanch and peel pearl onions for this salad. We don't recommend using frozen pearl onions.

Prep: 38 min.   Cook: 33 min.

2	(10-ounce) packages fresh pearl onions
1	head red cabbage, shredded
2	tablespoons salt
2	tablespoons olive oil
6	tablespoons white wine vinegar, divided
6	tablespoons maple syrup, divided
2	cups chopped pecans, toasted and divided
1	cup sour cream
½	teaspoon salt
4	Granny Smith apples, chopped
1	head curly endive, chopped

Trim bottom ends of onions. Blanch unpeeled onions, in batches, in rapidly boiling water in a large saucepan 45 seconds. (It's important to blanch in batches so that the water remains at a boil.) Drain and peel onions; place in a large zip-top freezer bag, seal, and refrigerate overnight, if desired.

Combine cabbage and 2 tablespoons salt in a large bowl; let stand 30 minutes, tossing occasionally. Rinse thoroughly, and drain well.

Combine onions and oil in a shallow roasting pan or a large cast-iron skillet; toss to coat. Spread onions in a single layer. Roast at 450° for 25 minutes or until browned, stirring after 20 minutes.

Combine ¼ cup each vinegar and maple syrup; add to roasted onions. Roast 5 more minutes or until slightly thickened and onions are glazed. Set aside.

Combine remaining 2 tablespoons vinegar, 2 tablespoons maple syrup, 1 cup chopped pecans, sour cream, and ½ teaspoon salt in a food processor or blender; process 1 to 2 minutes or until smooth. Cover and chill dressing overnight, if desired.

Toss together chopped apple, cabbage, and endive in a large bowl. Drizzle each serving with dressing, and top with roasted onions; sprinkle with remaining 1 cup pecans. Yield: 8 servings.

Make Ahead: Blanch and peel pearl onions a day ahead; store in refrigerator. Prepare dressing up to a day ahead, and store in refrigerator.

Coffee-Crusted Beef Wellingtons

Coffee gives classic beef Wellington an intriguing new flavor dimension. For the pastry wrap, we found puff pastry shells easier to work with than sheets. Follow our make-ahead steps that make this fancy entrée easy. You can freeze filets up to a month ahead, and bake them without thawing.

Prep: 58 min.   Cook: 1 hr., 11 min.   Other: 8 hrs.

2	teaspoons freshly ground coffee
1	teaspoon salt
¾	teaspoon pepper
¾	teaspoon garlic powder
8	(5- to 6-ounce) center-cut filet mignons (1½" thick)
1	tablespoon olive oil or vegetable oil
3	tablespoons butter or margarine
¼	cup finely chopped onion
¼	cup finely chopped carrot
¼	cup finely chopped celery
2	garlic cloves, minced
¾	cup Madeira
¾	cup freshly brewed coffee
½	cup beef broth
2	tablespoons butter or margarine
½	pound fresh mushrooms, minced
2	shallots, minced
½	teaspoon salt
½	teaspoon pepper
½	cup Madeira
8	frozen puff pastry shells, thawed (we tested with part of 2 Pepperidge Farm [10-ounce] packages)
1	large egg, lightly beaten
2	large eggs, lightly beaten
2	tablespoons butter
2½	tablespoons all-purpose flour
½	cup whipping cream
½	teaspoon salt

Garnishes: fresh rosemary, flat-leaf parsley, and thyme

wine advice

Offer both red and white. Put an assortment of bottles on your sideboard for guests to sample. Consider an Australian Shiraz or French Syrah; the full-bodied flavor of either partners well with this rich meal of beef Wellington. For a white wine, offer Gallo of Sonoma Chardonnay, lightly chilled.
Serve wine in fashionable tumblers. They're elegant, yet sturdier than stemmed glasses (see Where To Find It on page 171).

Combine first 4 ingredients; stir well. Pat filets dry. Coat both sides of filets with spice rub. Heat 1 tablespoon oil in a large skillet over medium-high heat until skillet is hot. Sear filets, in 2 batches, 1 to 1½ minutes on each side. Remove filets from skillet; place on a plate, and cover and chill until ready to assemble Wellingtons. (Don't clean skillet.)

While filets are chilling, melt 3 tablespoons butter in same skillet over medium-high heat. Add onion, carrot, celery, and garlic; sauté 5 minutes or until very tender. Add ¾ cup Madeira, brewed coffee, and broth; simmer 5 minutes. Remove from heat, and let cool. Transfer sauce to a 4-cup glass measuring cup, and chill overnight, if desired, or pour cooled sauce into ice cube trays and freeze. Once frozen, seal frozen sauce cubes in zip-top freezer bags.

Melt 2 tablespoons butter in same skillet over medium-high heat. Add mushrooms, shallots, ½ teaspoon salt, and ½ teaspoon pepper; sauté until all liquid evaporates. Add ½ cup Madeira; cook over medium-high heat until all liquid evaporates. Remove from heat, and let cool. Cover and chill until ready to assemble Wellingtons.

Roll each of 8 puff pastry shells to about ⅛" thick on a lightly floured surface; spoon 1 heaping tablespoonful mushroom filling in center of each pastry. Top each with a chilled filet. Brush edges of each pastry square with 1 beaten egg. Wrap 2 opposite sides of pastry over each filet, overlapping them; seal seam with beaten egg. Wrap remaining 2 sides of pastry over filet, and seal with beaten egg. Seal any gaps with beaten egg and press pastry around filet to enclose completely. Wrap Wellingtons individually in press-and-seal plastic wrap. Place wrapped Wellingtons in large zip-top freezer bags, and freeze overnight or up to 1 month.

To bake, place oven rack on lowest oven shelf; preheat oven to 425°. Place a broiler pan on oven rack; heat pan 5 minutes. Brush tops and sides of frozen Wellingtons with 2 beaten eggs. Carefully place frozen Wellingtons, seam side down, on preheated pan. Bake at 425° for 36 minutes.

While Wellingtons bake, melt 2 tablespoons butter in a saucepan over medium heat; add 2½ tablespoons flour and cook, stirring constantly, 1 minute. Add reserved Madeira sauce; cook, stirring constantly, over medium heat 6 to 8 minutes or until slightly thickened. (If using frozen Madeira sauce cubes, thaw cubes in a saucepan over medium heat before adding to flour mixture.) Stir in whipping cream; simmer 5 minutes or until desired thickness. Add ½ teaspoon salt. Remove from heat.

Arrange baked Wellingtons on a serving platter. Cut a small slit in top of each pastry, and tuck several sprigs of fresh herbs into each slit. Serve with Madeira sauce. Yield: 8 servings.

Note: You can bake beef Wellingtons the same day they're assembled. After wrapping beef filets in pastry, cover and chill Wellingtons 1 hour. Bake as directed above, reducing the baking time to 20 to 25 minutes.

worry-free Wellingtons

This update of a classic and time-consuming entrée has great merit for today's busy cook and host.

• You can assemble the pastry-wrapped beef, make the sauce ahead, and freeze both up to 1 month. The sauce freezes well in ice cube trays. Wrap the Wellingtons in press-and-seal plastic wrap and then in zip-top freezer bags.

• We found that preheating a broiler pan for 5 minutes and baking Wellingtons on the lowest oven shelf produced the best baked results with golden, flaky pastry.

• There's no fussy pastry cutout garnish. Before serving, simply tuck fresh herbs into the pastry for each serving.

Cast-Iron Herbed Potatoes Anna

Last-minute stovetop cooking gets this classic potato dish browned and crispy on the bottom. A well-seasoned cast-iron skillet is the key to unmolding the dish.

Prep: 27 min.   Cook: 1 hr., 17 min.

⅓   cup butter
6   garlic cloves, finely chopped
1   tablespoon finely chopped fresh rosemary
1   tablespoon finely chopped fresh thyme
2   tablespoons vegetable oil
2¼ pounds russet potatoes, peeled and thinly sliced
      (about ⅛" thick)
¾   teaspoon salt, divided
¾   teaspoon freshly ground pepper, divided

Melt butter in a small skillet over medium heat. Add garlic. Cook 2 minutes or just until garlic is lightly browned. Remove from heat, and stir in rosemary and thyme; set aside.

Brush bottom and sides of a 9" cast-iron skillet with 2 tablespoons oil. Arrange enough potato slices to cover bottom of skillet, overlapping slices; drizzle with one-third herbed garlic butter. Sprinkle with ¼ teaspoon salt and ¼ teaspoon pepper. Repeat procedure twice with remaining potato, herbed garlic butter, salt, and pepper. Brush a piece of aluminum foil with melted butter; press foil firmly, buttered side down, onto potato slices.

Bake at 400° for 1 hour and 10 minutes. Remove from oven, and using an oven mitt, press down firmly on the aluminum foil-covered potatoes. Remove aluminum foil, and place skillet on stovetop over medium heat. Cook 5 minutes. Remove from heat; let stand 2 minutes. Invert potatoes onto a plate, coaxing potatoes loose from skillet with a spatula. Yield: 6 to 8 servings.

Make Ahead: Bake potatoes Anna earlier in the day; invert onto an ovenproof plate, and cover loosely with foil. Just before serving, uncover and reheat at 400° for 10 minutes.

Carrots with Country Bacon

Carrots with Country Bacon

Country bacon in this recipe refers to thick-sliced or wood-smoked bacon.

Prep: 19 min.   Cook: 35 min.

4   thick bacon slices
2   pounds carrots, peeled and diagonally sliced into
      1" pieces
2   cups water
¼   cup firmly packed light brown sugar
2   tablespoons butter or margarine
2   teaspoons chopped fresh thyme

Cook bacon in a large skillet over medium heat until crisp. Drain, reserving 1 tablespoon drippings in skillet. Crumble bacon, and set aside. Add carrots and next 3 ingredients to skillet. Bring to a boil. Cook over medium-high heat 30 to 35 minutes or until liquid is reduced to a glaze and carrots are tender. Sprinkle with thyme and reserved bacon. Yield: 6 to 8 servings.

Make Ahead: Peel and slice carrots up to a day ahead. Store in a zip-top plastic bag in refrigerator.

Keep your centerpiece low
and simple.

Scalloped Greens

Greens have never tasted as good as they do in this crumb-topped casserole.

Prep: 28 min.   Cook: 3 hrs.   Other: 15 min.

1	(1-pound) bag chopped collard greens
1	(1-pound) bag chopped turnip greens
3	cups water
½	cup all-purpose flour
¼	cup grated onion
2	large garlic cloves, minced
3	cups milk
2	cups half-and-half
2	large eggs
1¼	teaspoons salt, divided
¼	teaspoon pepper
2	cups (8 ounces) shredded sharp white Cheddar cheese
2	cups (8 ounces) shredded Havarti cheese
3	cups sourdough breadcrumbs (see Note)
2	tablespoons butter or margarine, melted

Wash greens; remove coarse stems. Bring greens and water to a boil in a large Dutch oven. Cover, reduce heat, and simmer 1 hour and 45 minutes or until tender, stirring occasionally. Drain well. Return greens to pot.

Whisk together flour, next 5 ingredients, 1 teaspoon salt, and pepper. Add to greens in pot. Add cheeses; pour into a buttered 13" x 9" baking dish.

Combine breadcrumbs, 2 tablespoons melted butter, and remaining ¼ teaspoon salt, tossing until crumbs are coated. Sprinkle over greens.

Bake, uncovered, at 350° for 1 hour and 15 minutes or until golden. Let stand 15 minutes before serving. Yield: 15 servings.

Note: To make 3 cups sourdough breadcrumbs, we used ⅓ (10-ounce) round loaf sourdough bread, torn into pieces, and pulsed in a food processor.

Make Ahead: Cook greens, shred cheese, assemble casserole, and store in refrigerator, without breadcrumb topping, up to a day ahead. Prepare breadcrumb topping, and add just before baking. Bake casserole according to recipe up to 2 hours before serving. Reheat briefly before serving.

Cardamom-Scented Sweet Potato Pie

This delicately flavored custard pie is accented with freshly ground spices.

Prep: 19 min.   Cook: 1 hr., 28 min.

1¼	pounds sweet potatoes, peeled and cut into 1½" chunks
1	(3") cinnamon stick, broken
¼	teaspoon cardamom seeds
4	large eggs
2	cups half-and-half
1	cup sugar
2	teaspoons grated orange zest
2	teaspoons vanilla extract
¼	teaspoon salt
1½	cups all-purpose flour
½	teaspoon salt
½	cup chilled shortening
5 to 6	tablespoons ice water

Garnishes: sweetened whipped cream, ground cinnamon

Arrange sweet potato in a steamer basket over boiling water. Cover and steam 20 minutes or until very tender.

While sweet potato cooks, process cinnamon and cardamom seeds in a coffee grinder or blender until finely ground; set aside, reserving ¼ teaspoon for top of pie.

When sweet potato is done, cool slightly, and process in a food processor until smooth. Whisk together spices (except for ¼ teaspoon), sweet potato, eggs, and next 5 ingredients in a large bowl.

Combine flour and ½ teaspoon salt. Cut in shortening with a pastry blender until the size of small peas. Sprinkle ice water, 1 tablespoon at a time, evenly over surface; stir with a fork until dry ingredients are moistened. Shape dough into a ball. Roll dough to about ¼" thickness on a lightly floured surface. Fit into an ungreased 9½" deep-dish fluted tart pan; trim off excess pastry along edges. Line tart shell with aluminum foil, pressing foil into the flutes. Trim foil to within ½" of top of pan. Fold foil down over top edge of crust to prevent overbrowning.

Bake at 425° for 15 minutes; remove foil, and bake 7 minutes or until pastry is golden. Reduce oven temperature to 350°. With tart pan still on oven rack, pull out rack; pour filling into pastry, and sprinkle with remaining ¼ teaspoon spices. Bake at 350° for 1 hour or until set. Cool completely before serving. Garnish, if desired. Store in refrigerator. Yield: 1 (9½") deep-dish pie.

Cardamom-Scented Sweet Potato Pie

Note: If you don't have a fluted tart pan, you can bake this pie in 2 (9") glass pieplates. Fit each piecrust (from a 15-ounce package refrigerated piecrusts) into a 9" pieplate according to package directions; fold edges under, and crimp. (No need to prebake crusts for these smaller pies.) Pour filling evenly into 2 prepared piecrusts. Sprinkle with remaining ¼ teaspoon spices. Bake at 450° for 15 minutes.

Reduce heat to 350°; bake 30 more minutes or until set. Cool on a wire rack. (Pies will be thin.) Or bake pies using 2 frozen piecrusts.

Tip: Use a meat mallet to break cinnamon stick before placing in coffee grinder. Tap cardamom pods lightly with mallet to release seeds.

Use a sideboard to keep wine bottles, bread, the entrée platter, desserts, dessert plates, and coffee cups during the meal.

Chocolate Tiramisù Charlotte

Chocolate Tiramisù Charlotte

Every holiday dinner needs a luscious chocolate dessert. This one can be made ahead and can sit out awhile before serving.

Prep: 1 hr.   Cook: 14 min.   Other: 8 hrs., 20 min.

1	round bakery pound cake
2	tablespoons instant espresso granules
¾	cup boiling water
½	cup Kahlúa or sweet marsala wine, divided
6	large eggs, separated
1¼	cups sugar, divided
2	envelopes unflavored gelatin
½	cup cold water
½	cup whipping cream, divided
1½	(8-ounce) containers mascarpone cheese*
1¼	cups (8 ounces) double chocolate morsels, divided (we tested with Ghirardelli)
2	tablespoons butter

Garnishes: sweetened whipped cream, coarsely chopped chocolate-covered coffee beans

Slice enough pound cake to get 18 (⅓") slices. Line sides and bottom of an ungreased 9" springform pan with 12 to 14 slices of pound cake. Set remaining pound cake aside. Dissolve espresso in ¾ cup boiling water; stir in ¼ cup Kahlúa. Brush pound cake with ¾ cup espresso mixture, setting aside remaining ¼ cup espresso mixture.

Whisk together 6 egg whites and ¾ cup sugar in top of a double boiler; place over simmering water, and cook, whisking often, until mixture reaches 160°. Transfer egg white mixture to a large bowl; beat at high speed with an electric mixer until stiff peaks form. Set aside.

Sprinkle gelatin over ½ cup cold water in a saucepan; let soften 1 minute. Cook over medium heat, stirring until gelatin dissolves. Add ¼ cup whipping cream; set aside.

Whisk together 6 egg yolks, remaining ½ cup sugar, and remaining ¼ cup Kahlúa in top of double boiler. Place over simmering water, and cook, whisking often, until mixture reaches 160°. Remove bowl, and beat at medium speed with a handheld electric mixer until thick and pale. Add mascarpone cheese and gelatin mixture, beating until smooth. Fold in about 1 cup meringue; fold in remaining meringue. Spoon half of mascarpone mixture into springform pan. Top with remaining pound cake slices; brush pound cake slices with remaining ¼ cup espresso mixture.

Place half of chocolate morsels in a glass bowl. Microwave on HIGH 1½ minutes; stir until smooth and slightly cool. Add ½ cup mascarpone mixture, stirring until smooth; fold into remaining mascarpone mixture. Spoon chocolate mascarpone mixture into springform pan. Chill 20 minutes or until slightly firm on top.

Combine remaining chocolate morsels, remaining ¼ cup whipping cream, and butter in a small glass bowl. Microwave on HIGH 1½ minutes. Stir until chocolate melts and mixture is smooth. Spoon chocolate ganache over top of dessert, spreading to edges with a small offset spatula. Cover and chill at least 8 hours.

Before serving, run a knife around edge of pan to release sides. Remove Charlotte to a serving plate; let stand 20 minutes. Garnish, if desired. Yield: 12 servings.

*Substitute 12 ounces cream cheese if you can't find mascarpone cheese.

helping hands

The heart of the holiday season is spending time with loved ones. If you're hosting the holiday dinner, don't be shy about asking for help. Guests will enjoy being asked to pitch in for last-minute tasks like lighting candles, stirring gravy, opening or pouring wine, or serving up side dishes.

The Season's Best Recipes

Here, you'll find everything you need to make your holidays delicious. Enjoy some showstopping eggnog desserts, 5 ingredient 15 minute dishes, and party appetizers in a jiffy.

5 Ingredient 15 Minute Holiday Recipes

Get the festivities started with these simple and stylish recipes.

Warm Brie with Pear Preserves

What could be more enticing during the holidays than recipes with only five ingredients and 15 minutes of work time? We think you'll like this variety that includes sweet and savory, drink and dessert. We don't include salt, pepper, water, cooking spray, or garnish in the ingredient count. For speedy results with pasta and baked goods respectively, put your water on to boil and preheat the oven as your first step.

quick & easy
Warm Brie with Pear Preserves

Leaving the edible white rind on the Brie and cutting the cheese into wedges are two steps toward a quick finish. Serve Brie with thin gingersnaps, fruit, or crackers.

Prep: 10 min.   Cook: 4 min.

½   cup pear preserves
2   tablespoons sweet white wine (we tested with Riesling)
1½ teaspoons chopped fresh thyme or ½ teaspoon dried thyme
2   (8-ounce) rounds Brie
¼   cup chopped walnuts
Garnishes: fresh thyme sprigs, walnut halves

Combine first 3 ingredients in a small glass bowl; set bowl aside.

Cut each round of Brie into 6 wedges. Place wedges close together on a lightly greased baking sheet; sprinkle each round with 2 tablespoons chopped walnuts.

Bake at 450° for 4 minutes or just until cheese begins to soften in the center. Meanwhile, microwave preserves mixture on HIGH 20 seconds or just until thoroughly heated. Using 2 spatulas, carefully remove each Brie intact from baking sheet, and immediately place on a serving platter. Spoon melted preserves over Brie. Garnish, if desired. Serve hot. Yield: 12 servings.

Fix it Faster: Heat Brie with toppings, 1 round at a time, in the microwave on HIGH 1½ minutes on a microwave-safe plate. You don't even have to cut Brie into wedges.

quick & easy
Peppermint Patty Hot Chocolate

Garnishes make this drink fun to serve. For children, omit the peppermint schnapps.

Prep: 1 min.   Cook: 13 min.

4   cups milk
4   cups whipping cream
½   cup sugar
3   (4-ounce) semisweet chocolate baking bars, broken into pieces (we tested with Ghirardelli)
¼   teaspoon salt
¾   cup peppermint schnapps
Garnishes: canned whipped topping, crushed hard peppermint candies

Heat first 3 ingredients in a large saucepan over medium-high heat until sugar dissolves and mixture is thoroughly heated. Remove from heat; add chocolate and salt, whisking until chocolate melts. Stir in peppermint schnapps. Garnish, if desired. Serve immediately. Yield: 11 cups.

Note: For added indulgence, dip a peppermint patty lollipop into hot chocolate. It will partially melt and add an extra peppermint punch. We tested with peppermint patty candies and 4" and 6" white lollipop sticks.

Peppermint Patty
Hot Chocolate

Banana Bread French Toast

❄ *quick & easy*
Banana Bread French Toast

Serve warm with your favorite syrup.

Prep: 2 min.   Cook: 13 min.

4   large eggs, lightly beaten
1   cup milk
3   tablespoons butter or margarine
1   (16-ounce) loaf banana crunch swirl bread (we
    tested with Cobblestone Mill Breakfast Swirl)
Toppings: chopped pecans, sliced banana

Whisk together eggs and milk.

Melt 1½ tablespoons butter in a large nonstick skillet over medium-high heat. Lightly dip bread slices, 1 at a time, in egg mixture. Cook bread slices, in batches, 2 to 3 minutes on each side or until golden. Add remaining butter to skillet as needed.

Top each serving with pecans and sliced banana, if desired. Serve hot. Yield: 4 to 5 servings.

Spicy Queso Dip

This is no ordinary cheese dip. It's chock-full of spinach, sausage, black beans, and green chiles.

Prep: 3 min.   Cook: 9 min.

1   (16-ounce) package mild ground pork sausage
2   (16-ounce) cartons refrigerated hot queso dip (we tested with Gordo's Cheese Dip)
1   (10-ounce) package frozen chopped spinach, thawed and well drained
1   (15-ounce) can black beans, drained
1   (10-ounce) can diced tomatoes and green chiles, undrained

Cook sausage in a large skillet over medium-high heat, stirring until sausage crumbles and is no longer pink. Drain.

Meanwhile, heat queso dip according to package microwave directions in a 2-quart microwave-safe bowl. Stir in sausage, spinach, and beans. Drain tomatoes and green chiles, reserving juice. Add tomatoes and green chiles to dip. Stir in enough reserved juice to get a good consistency (about 2 to 3 tablespoons). Serve hot with tortilla chips. Yield: 7½ cups.

Chicken and Prosciutto Pasta with Sage Butter

Fresh sage and portobello mushrooms give this simple dish robust flavor. For quick results, put the water on to boil right as you begin.

Prep: 7 min.   Cook: 15 min.

2   (9-ounce) packages refrigerated chicken and prosciutto tortellini (we tested with Buitoni)
½   cup butter, divided
2   (8-ounce) packages baby portobello or cremini mushrooms, sliced (about 6 cups)
1½ tablespoons chopped fresh sage
1   cup freshly grated Asiago or Parmesan cheese

Cook tortellini according to package directions; drain. Return pasta to warm pot.

While pasta cooks, melt ¼ cup butter in a large skillet over medium-high heat. Add mushrooms, and sauté 3 minutes or until tender. Remove from heat; add to pasta.

Heat remaining ¼ cup butter in a small microwave-safe bowl on HIGH 30 seconds or until butter melts. Stir in sage. Add to pasta. Sprinkle with grated cheese; toss and serve immediately. Yield: 4 servings.

Peppered Beef Fillets with Pomegranate Jus

The 1-inch thickness of the fillets is important for uniform cooking. Press fillets with the palm of your hand to make fillet thickness match.

Prep: 4 min.   Cook: 12 min.

6   beef tenderloin fillets (about 1" thick)
¼   teaspoon salt
¼   cup au poivre marinade, divided (see Note)
⅔   cup minced onion or shallot
⅔   cup refrigerated pomegranate juice or red wine
3   ounces Gorgonzola or blue cheese

Sprinkle fillets evenly with salt. Rub fillets with 3 tablespoons au poivre marinade. Place a large nonstick skillet over medium-high heat until hot. Add fillets, and cook 5 minutes on each side or until desired degree of doneness. Remove fillets from skillet, and keep warm.

Add remaining 1 tablespoon au poivre marinade to skillet. Add onion, and sauté 30 seconds, scraping browned bits from bottom of skillet. Add pomegranate juice. Bring to a boil, and cook 1 minute.

To serve, pour pomegranate jus over fillets, and top each serving with cheese. Yield: 6 servings.

Note: We tested with LuLu Au Poivre marinade from Williams-Sonoma. You can otherwise use our similar homemade marinade. Combine ¼ cup extra-virgin olive oil, 1½ teaspoons cracked black pepper, 1 teaspoon each dried parsley flakes and dried oregano, ¼ teaspoon fine-grained sea salt, and 1 large garlic clove, pressed.

Pork Chops with
Shallot-Cranberry
Sauce

Pork Chops with Shallot-Cranberry Sauce

For an easy and impressive presentation, perch these skillet chops on a mound of mashed potatoes.

Prep: 7 min.   Cook: 13 min.

4   boneless pork loin chops (¾" thick)
¾   teaspoon salt, divided
½   teaspoon freshly ground black pepper
2   tablespoons butter, divided
2   shallots, finely chopped (¼ cup)
1   (12-ounce) container cranberry-orange crushed fruit
1½ teaspoons chopped fresh thyme
Garnish: fresh thyme

Sprinkle both sides of pork with ½ teaspoon salt and pepper. Melt 1 tablespoon butter in a large skillet over medium-high heat. Add pork, and cook 4 to 5 minutes on each side or to desired degree of doneness. Remove pork from skillet; cover and keep warm.

Add remaining 1 tablespoon butter to skillet, stirring just until butter melts. Add shallots, and sauté 1 to 2 minutes. Add crushed fruit and remaining ¼ teaspoon salt to skillet; bring to a boil. Return pork and any juices to skillet; cook 1 minute or until heated. Sprinkle with chopped thyme, and serve hot. Garnish, if desired. Yield: 4 servings.

Sweet Potato Soup

Ground red pepper puts a spicy kick in this soup. The soup is good without the pepper, too.

Prep: 10 min.   Cook: 5 min.

1   (40-ounce) can yams in heavy syrup
1   (14-ounce) can vegetable or chicken broth
½   cup fresh orange juice
1 to 2 tablespoons minced fresh ginger
1½ cups coconut milk (we tested with Taste of Thai)
1   teaspoon salt
¼   teaspoon ground red pepper

Drain yams, reserving ½ cup syrup. Discard remaining syrup. Place yams in a blender or food processor. Add ½ cup syrup, broth, orange juice, and ginger. Process 2 to 3 minutes or until smooth, stopping to scrape down sides.

Pour pureed mixture into a medium saucepan. Stir in coconut milk and remaining ingredients. Cook over medium heat, stirring often, until soup is thoroughly heated. Ladle soup into bowls. If desired, drizzle additional coconut milk into soup. Run a knife through each bowl to make a decorative design. Yield: 6 cups.

Rosemary Roasted Grape Tomatoes

These tiny tomatoes take on a sweetness when roasted. Serve them as a simple side dish, or toss with hot cooked pasta.

Prep: 5 min.   Cook: 8 min.

2   pints grape tomatoes
1   tablespoon chopped fresh or dried rosemary
1   tablespoon olive oil
½   teaspoon salt
½   teaspoon freshly ground pepper
Garnish: fresh rosemary sprigs

Rinse tomatoes, and pat dry with paper towels.

Combine tomatoes and next 4 ingredients; toss gently to coat. Place tomatoes in a single layer in a shallow roasting pan.

Bake at 475° for 7 to 8 minutes or until tomato skins are blistered and start to pop, stirring once. Garnish, if desired. Yield: 4 servings.

❄ *make ahead* • *quick & easy*

Caramel-Chocolate Tartlets

Dulce de leche is a fancy name for caramel. It makes these bite-size sweets really rich.

Prep: 14 min. Other: 1 min.

1   (13.4-ounce) can dulce de leche (we tested with Nestlé)*
2   (2.1-ounce) packages frozen mini phyllo pastry shells, thawed (we tested with Athens)
1   cup double chocolate morsels (we tested with Ghirardelli) or regular semisweet morsels
⅓   cup roasted salted peanuts, chopped, or coarsely chopped pecans, or both

Spoon 1 heaping teaspoon dulce de leche into each pastry shell. Microwave chocolate morsels in a small glass bowl on HIGH 1 to 1½ minutes or until melted, stirring twice. Spoon 1 teaspoon chocolate over dulce de leche. Sprinkle tartlets with peanuts or pecans. Freeze 1 minute to set chocolate. Yield: 30 tartlets.

Tip: Make the tartlets ahead, and freeze them in the plastic pastry trays sealed in zip-top freezer bags.

*Find dulce de leche on the baking aisle or the Mexican food aisle or make your own. Pour 1 (14-ounce) can sweetened condensed milk into an 8" dish or pieplate; cover with foil. Pour ½" hot water into a larger pan. Place covered pieplate in pan. Bake at 425° for 1 hour and 25 minutes or until thick and caramel colored (add hot water to pan as needed). Remove foil when done; cool.

preparing Caramel-Chocolate Tartlets

• Spoon 1 heaping teaspoon dulce de leche into each pastry shell.

• Keep tartlets in pastry trays, and freeze in zip-top bags.

make ahead

Banana Cream Cake

We liked this cake served partially frozen. We found bakery pound cake easiest to slice when it's partially frozen, too.

Prep: 15 min.   Other: 2 hrs.

1   round bakery pound cake (about 3 pounds)
1   (15.6-ounce) jar banana jam*
3   large bananas, sliced and divided
1   (12-ounce) container frozen whipped topping, thawed
1   cup chopped pecans
Garnish: 3 (1.4-ounce) chocolate-covered toffee candy bars, chopped

Turn cake on its side, and slice evenly into 3 layers.

Place bottom layer on a serving platter. Spread with 3 tablespoons banana jam. Top with half of banana slices. Spread ½ cup whipped topping over banana slices; sprinkle with ¼ cup pecans. Top with second cake layer. Repeat layering ingredients; top with remaining cake layer.

Frost assembled cake with remaining whipped topping. Sprinkle remaining pecans over cake. Garnish, if desired. Serve right away or cover and chill until ready to serve, or freeze cake 2 hours if you want to serve it partially frozen. Yield: 1 (3-layer) cake.

*We used banana jam from Williams-Sonoma. Serve leftover jam on toast or biscuits. If you can't find banana jam, use mashed ripe banana sweetened with a touch of honey.

Banana Cream Cake

Ambrosia Trifle

❄ *quick & easy • make ahead*

Ambrosia Trifle

Layer these ingredients in one big bowl or several small hurricane glasses that each hold two servings.

Prep: 7 min. Cook: 8 min.

1   cup sweetened flaked coconut
1   (24-ounce) package prepared vanilla pudding (we tested with Jello Pudding Snacks)*
1   (8-ounce) container frozen creamy whipped topping, thawed and divided
2   (24-ounce) jars refrigerated mandarin oranges (we tested with Del Monte Sun Fresh)
½   round bakery pound cake, cut into 1" cubes

Place coconut on a baking sheet. Bake at 350° for 8 minutes or until lightly browned; set aside.

Meanwhile, stir together pudding and 1½ cups whipped topping. Drain oranges, reserving liquid.

Layer half of cake cubes in 6 (2-cup) stemmed glasses or a 3-quart glass bowl or trifle dish. Brush cake cubes with reserved liquid; spoon half of pudding evenly over cubes. Top with half of oranges. Repeat layers, ending with oranges. Dollop with desired amount of whipped topping; sprinkle with toasted coconut. Chill until ready to serve. Yield: 10 to 12 servings.

*As an option, you can use a (5.1-ounce) package vanilla instant pudding that yields about 3 cups.

For the Love of Eggnog

*The velvety smooth holiday drink becomes
a key ingredient in these recipes.*

Hazelnut-Eggnog
Punch

❄️*editor's favorite*

Hazelnut-Eggnog Punch

Serve this as a luscious dessert drink.

Prep: 7 min.   Other: 1 hr., 15 min.

2   cups milk
1   vanilla bean, split lengthwise
1   (3") cinnamon stick
6   cups refrigerated or canned eggnog
1½   cups Frangelico or other hazelnut liqueur
1   cup whipping cream, whipped
1   quart vanilla ice cream, softened
Grated nutmeg (optional)

Combine first 3 ingredients in a small saucepan; place over medium heat, and cook until hot (do not boil), stirring often. Remove from heat. Cover and let stand 30 minutes. Scrape vanilla bean seeds into milk mixture. Cover and chill. Discard vanilla bean and cinnamon stick.

Combine chilled milk mixture, eggnog, and Frangelico in a punch bowl; fold in whipped cream. Scoop ice cream into punch; stir gently. Sprinkle lightly with nutmeg, if desired. Yield: 15 cups.

❄️*make ahead*

Eggnog Panna Cotta

Panna cotta is a light, silky smooth Italian custard. This version gets a dark caramel glaze.

Prep: 6 min.   Cook: 12 min.   Other: 8 hrs.

3   cups refrigerated or canned eggnog
¼   teaspoon freshly grated nutmeg
1   envelope unflavored gelatin
¼   cup cold water
1   teaspoon clear vanilla extract
½   cup unsalted butter
½   cup firmly packed dark brown sugar
⅛   teaspoon salt
¼   cup dark rum

Coat 6 (4-ounce) ramekins or 6-ounce custard cups with vegetable cooking spray. Set aside.

Combine eggnog and nutmeg in a medium saucepan; bring to a simmer over medium heat, stirring often. Meanwhile, sprinkle gelatin over cold water in a large bowl; let stand 1 minute. Remove eggnog from heat; stir in vanilla.

our test kitchens' eggnog tips

After testing dozens of holiday recipes using canned and refrigerated eggnog, our staff decided we had definite opinions about the creamy drink as an ingredient. Here's our best advice this holiday season.

Freezing eggnog works like a charm. Buy eggnog after Christmas when store owners are ready to restock. For eggnog that comes in a carton, freeze it in its original carton up to 1 year. When ready to use, thaw frozen eggnog in the refrigerator overnight, and shake it well before opening. Keep canned, unopened eggnog in a cool dark spot in the pantry up to 18 months.

Eggnog as an ingredient gives great flavor to desserts. In testing, we found that store-bought eggnog's slight cinnamon flavor and creamy texture add depth to a variety of desserts, especially ice cream. We don't recommend substituting low-fat refrigerated eggnog in any of these recipes.

Refrigerated eggnog tastes best. We prefer the refrigerated eggnog that comes in a carton versus canned eggnog (although canned tends to be more readily available). The refrigerated version has a richer consistency and more flecks of spice. We suggest using the refrigerated eggnog for many of the following recipes, but they'll work just fine if canned eggnog is what's available.

Rich memories can linger. Follow our freezing advice above to enjoy these eggnog recipes year-round and to keep the thoughts and tastes of Christmas alive throughout the year.

Gradually whisk hot eggnog mixture into softened gelatin, stirring until gelatin dissolves. Pour ½ cup custard mixture into each ramekin. Cover and chill 8 hours.

Melt butter in a small heavy saucepan over medium heat. Gradually add sugar and salt; cook 8 minutes or until sugar dissolves and mixture is smooth, whisking constantly. Remove from heat; whisk in rum. Cover and chill.

To serve, gently invert each panna cotta onto a dessert plate. Drizzle each dessert plate with chilled rum sauce. Serve immediately. Yield: 6 servings.

Eggnog Fudge

Eggnog Fudge

Candied cherries and toasted nuts flavor this creamy fudge.

Prep: 13 min. Cook: 19 min. Other: 18 min.

2   cups sugar
1   cup refrigerated eggnog
2   tablespoons butter
2   tablespoons light corn syrup
¼   cup chopped pecans, toasted
¼   cup slivered almonds, toasted and chopped
½   cup chopped red candied cherries
1   teaspoon vanilla extract

Line an 8" x 4" loafpan with aluminum foil; butter foil, and set aside.

Combine first 4 ingredients in a 4-quart heavy saucepan. Cook over medium heat, stirring constantly, until mixture comes to a boil. Wash down crystals from sides of pan, using a pastry brush dipped in hot water. Insert a candy thermometer into eggnog mixture. Cook, stirring occasionally, until thermometer registers 238°. Remove from heat and cool, undisturbed, until temperature drops to 190° (15 to 18 minutes).

Stir in pecans and remaining 3 ingredients; beat with a wooden spoon until fudge thickens and just begins to lose its gloss (5 to 8 minutes). Pour candy into prepared pan. Cool completely; cut into squares. Yield: about 1½ pounds.

Creamy Eggnog Ice Cream

Prep: 10 min. Cook: 25 min. Other: 2 hrs., 50 min.

2   cups milk
1   vanilla bean, split lengthwise
8   egg yolks
1   cup sugar
1½   teaspoons ground cinnamon
½   teaspoon ground nutmeg
½   teaspoon salt
3   cups whipping cream
1   cup refrigerated eggnog

Cook milk in a heavy saucepan over medium heat, stirring often, just until bubbles appear; remove from heat. Add vanilla bean; cover and let stand 20 minutes. Remove vanilla bean from milk; using the tip of a small sharp knife, scrape vanilla bean seeds into milk. Discard vanilla bean pod.

Whisk together egg yolks and next 4 ingredients in a large bowl until thickened. Gradually whisk warm vanilla milk into yolk mixture; return to saucepan.

Cook over low heat, whisking constantly, 20 minutes or until a thermometer registers 160° and custard coats a spoon. Remove from heat; pour through a wire-mesh strainer into a bowl. Cool at room temperature about 30 minutes, stirring occasionally. Stir in whipping cream and eggnog; cover and chill 1 hour.

Pour custard mixture into freezer container of a 1-gallon hand-turned or electric freezer. Freeze according to manufacturer's instructions. Pack freezer with additional ice and rock salt; let stand 1 hour before serving. Yield: about 2 quarts.

Creamy Eggnog Ice Cream

❄ *make ahead*

Belgian Waffles with Eggnog Butter and Orange Syrup

Make these waffles ahead, and freeze them. Reheat in a toaster to recrisp them.

Prep: 8 min.   Cook: 52 min.   Other: 8 hrs.

2⅔ cups all-purpose flour
2 tablespoons sugar
1 teaspoon salt
1 (¼-ounce) envelope active dry yeast
1¾ cups milk
¼ cup water
¼ cup butter or margarine, softened
3 large eggs
Eggnog Butter
Orange Syrup

Belgian Waffles with Eggnog Butter and Orange Syrup

Stir together first 4 ingredients in a large bowl; set aside.

Combine milk, water, and butter in a 4-cup glass measuring cup; microwave on HIGH 1½ minutes or until mixture reaches 120° to 130°.

Add milk mixture to dry ingredients alternately with eggs, beating at medium speed with an electric mixer just until dry ingredients are blended. Cover and chill batter 8 hours.

Pour batter, 1 cup at a time, into a preheated, oiled waffle iron; cook until golden. Serve warm with Eggnog Butter and Orange Syrup. Yield: 16 (4") waffles.

eggnog butter

This flavored butter can be made ahead. Soften butter at room temperature before serving.

Prep: 5 min.

1 cup butter, softened
½ cup sifted powdered sugar
½ teaspoon ground nutmeg
1 teaspoon rum extract
½ teaspoon vanilla extract

Beat butter at high speed with an electric mixer until creamy. Gradually add powdered sugar, beating well. Stir in nutmeg and extracts. Cover and chill. Yield: 1¼ cups.

orange syrup

Syrup can be made ahead and reheated in the microwave before serving.

Prep: 1 min.   Cook: 5 min.

1 cup pure maple syrup
½ cup orange marmalade

Combine syrup and marmalade in a small saucepan over medium heat. Cook until mixture comes to a simmer and marmalade melts, about 5 minutes. Yield: 1½ cups.

Note: We tested with a Belgian Waffle iron. For each batch, we used 1 cup batter and cooked 4 (4") waffles.

Fix it Faster: Buy frozen waffles, and top them with the Eggnog Butter and Orange Syrup.

Bread Pudding with White Chocolate-Brandied Eggnog Sauce

Our staff declared this one of the best bread puddings around, mainly because of the yummy sauce.

Prep: 16 min.   Cook: 1 hr., 5 min.   Other: 1 hr., 5 min.

1½ (1-pound) loaves cinnamon-raisin bread, cubed
½ cup chopped pecans, toasted
4 large eggs, lightly beaten
2 cups milk
2 cups whipping cream
½ cup granulated sugar
½ cup firmly packed light brown sugar
3 tablespoons butter or margarine, melted
1 teaspoon ground cinnamon
½ teaspoon ground nutmeg
1 teaspoon vanilla extract
White Chocolate-Brandied Eggnog Sauce

Arrange bread cubes in a lightly greased 13" x 9" baking dish; sprinkle pecans over bread cubes.

Whisk together eggs and next 8 ingredients. Pour egg mixture over bread cubes, pressing down cubes gently to absorb liquid. Cover and chill 1 hour.

Bake at 350° for 1 hour and 5 minutes or until a knife inserted in center comes out clean, shielding with aluminum foil after 30 minutes to prevent excessive browning. Let stand 5 minutes before serving. Serve warm with warm White Chocolate-Brandied Eggnog Sauce. Yield: 8 to 10 servings.

white chocolate-brandied eggnog sauce

Prep: 2 min.   Cook: 8 min.

½ cup sugar
½ cup butter
½ cup refrigerated eggnog
½ cup whipping cream
1½ teaspoons cornstarch
¼ cup water
1 (4-ounce) white chocolate baking bar, chopped (we tested with Ghirardelli)
2 tablespoons brandy (optional)

Combine first 4 ingredients in a heavy saucepan; cook over low heat 5 minutes or until sugar dissolves and butter melts, stirring occasionally.

Combine cornstarch and water; stir into eggnog mixture. Bring to a boil; boil 1 minute, stirring constantly. Remove from heat. Add white chocolate, stirring until chocolate melts. Stir in brandy, if desired. Serve warm. Yield: 2¾ cups.

Spiced Eggnog Pound Cake

Cake flour gives this cake its light texture. For a splurge, serve cake with Creamy Eggnog Ice Cream on page 142.

Prep: 25 min.   Cook: 55 min.   Other: 15 min.

1 cup butter, softened
3 cups granulated sugar
6 large eggs
3 cups sifted cake flour
¾ teaspoon baking powder
½ teaspoon salt
1 cup refrigerated or canned eggnog
2 teaspoons vanilla extract
2 tablespoons brandy (optional)
1 teaspoon ground cinnamon
¾ teaspoon freshly grated nutmeg
½ teaspoon ground allspice
¼ teaspoon ground cloves
Powdered sugar
1 cup sifted powdered sugar
2 tablespoons plus 1 teaspoon whipping cream

Generously grease and flour a 12-cup Bundt pan; set aside.

Beat butter at medium speed with an electric mixer about 2 minutes or until creamy. Gradually add granulated sugar, beating 5 to 7 minutes. Add eggs, 1 at a time, beating just until yellow disappears.

Combine flour, baking powder, and salt. Add to butter mixture alternately with 1 cup eggnog, beginning and ending with flour mixture. Beat at low speed just until blended after each addition. Stir in vanilla and, if desired, brandy.

Pour half of batter into prepared pan. Stir cinnamon and next 3 ingredients into remaining batter. Spoon spice batter over plain batter. Swirl batters together, using a knife.

Bake at 350° for 50 to 55 minutes or until a long wooden pick inserted in center comes out clean. Cool in pan on a wire rack 15 minutes. Remove from pan; cool on wire rack.

Place cake on a cake plate; dust with powdered sugar.

Combine 1 cup powdered sugar and whipping cream, stirring until smooth. Drizzle glaze over cake. Yield: 16 servings.

Spiced Eggnog Pound Cake

make ahead

Frozen White Chocolate Terrine with a Pistachio Crust

Make this festive frozen dessert in a loafpan or individual muffin cups.

Prep: 17 min. Cook: 10 min. Other: 8 hrs., 10 min.

1   cup shelled pistachio nuts
¼   cup graham cracker crumbs
2   tablespoons butter or margarine, melted
1   tablespoon sugar
9   ounces white chocolate, chopped
1   cup refrigerated or canned eggnog
1   teaspoon clear vanilla extract
1½   teaspoons rum extract
1   cup whipping cream

Line an 8½" x 4½" loafpan with a smooth piece of foil; butter bottom of foil-lined pan.

Process first 4 ingredients in a food processor until blended; press crumb crust into bottom of prepared pan. Bake at 350° for 7 minutes. Cool completely on a wire rack.

Place chopped white chocolate in a metal bowl.

Bring eggnog to a simmer in a small saucepan over medium heat. Pour hot eggnog over chopped white chocolate, stirring gently until blended and smooth. Stir in extracts. Chill white chocolate mixture over a large bowl of ice water 10 minutes or until slightly chilled, stirring occasionally.

Beat whipping cream at high speed with an electric mixer until stiff peaks form. Gradually fold whipped cream into chilled white chocolate mixture; pour over crust in pan. Cover and freeze 8 hours or until firm.

To serve, invert frozen terrine onto a cutting board; carefully remove foil. Cut terrine into 1"-thick slices. Serve immediately. Yield: 8 servings.

Mini White Chocolate Terrines: Cut crust ingredients in half. Place foil baking cups in muffin pans; butter baking cups. Press 1 tablespoon pistachio crust mixture into bottom of each cup. Bake at 350° for 5 minutes. Cool completely. Fill each cup with ⅓ cup white chocolate filling. Cover and freeze as directed above. To serve, carefully remove foil lining from each terrine, and invert onto serving plates. Serve immediately. Yield: 1 dozen.

make ahead

Toasted Coconut-Eggnog Cheesecake

Any type of rum can be substituted for dark rum in this recipe.

Prep: 21 min. Cook: 1 hr., 14 min. Other: 8 hrs.

1¼   cups sweetened flaked coconut
12   vanilla cream sandwich cookies, broken into pieces (we tested with Vienna Fingers)
½   cup chopped pecans, toasted
¼   cup butter or margarine, melted
4   (8-ounce) packages cream cheese, softened
1   cup sugar
½   cup refrigerated eggnog
1   tablespoon cornstarch
1   teaspoon ground cinnamon
¼   teaspoon ground nutmeg
2   tablespoons dark rum
4   large eggs
1   teaspoon vanilla extract
Garnishes: sweetened whipped cream, ground cinnamon

Bake 1¼ cups coconut in a shallow pan at 350°, stirring occasionally, 8 to 9 minutes or until toasted. Reserve ¼ cup for garnish.

Process cookies and pecans in a food processor until cookies are finely crushed. Add butter; pulse until crumbs are moistened. Add 1 cup toasted coconut; pulse just until combined. Press crumb mixture into bottom and 1" up sides of a 9" springform pan.

Bake at 350° for 10 minutes; let cool. Reduce oven temperature to 325°.

Meanwhile, beat cream cheese at medium speed with an electric mixer until creamy; gradually add sugar, beating well. Add eggnog and next 4 ingredients, beating just until combined. Add eggs, 1 at a time, beating just until yellow disappears. Stir in vanilla. (Do not overbeat.) Pour batter into baked crust.

Bake at 325° for 55 minutes or until set. Remove from oven, and immediately run a knife around edge of pan, releasing sides.

Cool completely in pan on a wire rack. Cover and chill 8 hours. Garnish, if desired. Sprinkle with reserved ¼ cup toasted coconut. Yield: 10 to 12 servings.

*Toasted Coconut-
Eggnog Cheesecake*

Eggnog Soufflés with Rum Crème Anglaise

These soufflés can be frozen ahead and then placed in the oven during dinner. Rum Crème Anglaise is also good served with fruit or waffles.

Prep: 19 min.   Cook: 43 min.   Other: 20 min.

1	tablespoon butter, softened
2	tablespoons granulated sugar
6	tablespoons butter
3	tablespoons all-purpose flour
½	teaspoon freshly grated nutmeg
¼	teaspoon ground cardamom
¾	cup half-and-half
½	cup granulated sugar
5	large eggs, separated
1	tablespoon vanilla extract
⅛	teaspoon salt
¼	teaspoon cream of tartar

Sifted powdered sugar
Rum Crème Anglaise

Butter bottom and sides of 6 (6-ounce) ramekins; sprinkle with 2 tablespoons sugar. Set aside.

Melt 6 tablespoons butter in a heavy saucepan over medium heat. Add flour, nutmeg, and cardamom, stirring until smooth. Cook 2 minutes, stirring constantly. Whisk in half-and-half and ½ cup granulated sugar; cook over medium heat 6 to 8 minutes, stirring constantly, until thickened. Remove from heat, and set aside.

Beat egg yolks at high speed with an electric mixer until thick and pale. Gradually stir about half of hot mixture into egg yolks. Add egg yolk mixture back to pan; cook over medium heat 2 minutes, stirring constantly, until thickened. Remove from heat; stir in vanilla. Set aside to cool 10 to 20 minutes.

Beat egg whites and salt in a large bowl at high speed until foamy. Add cream of tartar, beating until soft peaks form. Gradually fold beaten egg whites into custard mixture. Spoon into prepared ramekins, and place on a baking sheet. (Or cover and freeze soufflés up to 2 weeks.)

Bake at 350° for 30 minutes or until puffed and set. Sprinkle with powdered sugar; serve immediately with Rum Crème Anglaise. Yield: 6 servings.

Note: If freezing soufflés, let stand at room temperature 30 minutes before baking.

rum crème anglaise

Prep: 5 min.   Cook: 30 min.

2	cups half-and-half
½	vanilla bean, split lengthwise
5	egg yolks
½	cup sugar
2	tablespoons rum or spiced rum

Place half-and-half and vanilla bean in a heavy saucepan; bring just to a boil. Remove from heat; with the tip of a small sharp knife, scrape vanilla bean seeds into half-and-half, and discard pod.

Combine egg yolks and sugar in a large bowl; gradually whisk in hot half-and-half. Add yolk mixture back to pan, and cook, stirring constantly, until custard thickens and coats a spoon. Do not boil. Pour custard through a wire-mesh strainer into a bowl, and cool. Stir in rum. Cover and chill. Yield: 2 cups.

Eggnog Soufflés with Rum Crème Anglaise

Cheesecake Swirl Bars

Cheesecake Swirl Bars

*Cheesecake brownies get a splash of rum flavor. Cut them
into large bars for a special occasion splurge.*

Prep: 26 min.   Cook: 41 min.   Other: 1 hr.

55   vanilla wafers, crushed (2 cups)
6   tablespoons butter or margarine, melted
½   cup finely chopped pecans, toasted
2   (8-ounce) packages cream cheese, softened
½   cup sugar
1½   teaspoons rum extract
2   large eggs
¼   cup refrigerated eggnog
½   cup white chocolate morsels, melted
½   cup double chocolate morsels, melted (we tested
      with Ghirardelli), or regular semisweet morsels

Combine first 3 ingredients in a large bowl, stirring until
blended. Press crumb mixture into bottom of a lightly greased
8" or 9" square pan. Bake at 350° for 8 minutes. Cool.

Beat cream cheese, sugar, and rum extract at medium
speed with an electric mixer just until smooth. Add eggs,
1 at a time, beating just until blended. Pour 1½ cups cream
cheese batter evenly over baked crust.

Stir eggnog into remaining batter. Divide batter in half;
stir melted white chocolate into 1 portion. Spoon evenly
over cream cheese batter. Stir melted semisweet chocolate
into remaining batter. Drop spoonfuls of chocolate batter
evenly over white chocolate layer; gently swirl batters with
a knife.

Bake at 350° for 30 to 33 minutes or until almost set.
Cool completely on a wire rack. Cover and chill at least
1 hour before serving. Cut into bars. Yield: 1 dozen.

*Croquembouche
Christmas Tree*

Croquembouche (kroh-kuhm-BOOSH) is French for "crunch in the mouth." We've simplified this classic cream puff tree by using melted white chocolate as the "glue."

Croquembouche Christmas Tree

This is the ultimate grand dessert. Don't be intimidated by the length of the recipe; almost everything can be made in advance and assembled a few hours before serving.

Prep: 1 hr., 6 min. **Cook:** 41 min. **Other:** 2 hrs., 35 min.

Eggnog Pastry Cream

1½ cups water
¾ cup butter
1½ cups all-purpose flour
¼ teaspoon salt
6 large eggs
1 (9" or 12") white plastic craft foam cone
6 (4-ounce) packages white chocolate baking bars, coarsely chopped (we tested with Ghirardelli)
1 tablespoon plus 1 teaspoon shortening
Garnishes: silver and white edible glitter

Prepare Eggnog Pastry Cream; cover and chill.

Combine water and butter in a heavy saucepan; bring to a boil over medium-high heat. Add flour and salt all at once, stirring vigorously with a wooden spoon until mixture leaves sides of pan and forms a smooth ball. Remove from heat, and cool 5 minutes.

Add eggs, 1 at a time, beating well with a wooden spoon after each addition; then beat until dough is smooth.

Drop cream puff paste by rounded teaspoonfuls 2" apart onto ungreased baking sheets; then quickly smooth tops with the back of a spoon or wet fingers to round puffs.

Bake at 425° for 10 minutes. Reduce oven temperature to 400°, and switch positions of baking sheets. Bake 18 to 20 more minutes or until puffed and golden, switching position of baking sheets again halfway through baking. Turn off oven; let puffs stand in oven to dry 15 minutes. Remove puffs to wire racks to cool completely.

Pipe Eggnog Pastry Cream through side of each cream puff, using a pastry bag fitted with a long, narrow round tip. (We tested with a #10 round tip.)

Wrap cone with white parchment paper; secure paper onto cone with straight pins. Otherwise wrap cone in plastic wrap. Place cone on a large serving platter.

Melt chopped white chocolate bars and shortening in a heavy saucepan over low heat, stirring until smooth. Remove from heat.

Working with tongs, dip bottom of each cream puff, 1 at a time, into melted white chocolate. Starting at the base,

position enough cream puffs, side by side, on platter surrounding cone to form a ring. Add a second layer of cream puffs outside the first ring of puffs. Begin stacking rings of cream puffs, reducing the number on each layer so that it forms a pyramid (and hugs the cone). Reheat white chocolate over low heat, if necessary.

Drizzle any remaining white chocolate over finished tree. Sprinkle with edible glitter, if desired. Chill up to 2 hours before serving to set chocolate. Serve with small tongs. **Yield:** 85 cream puffs.

Note: The puffs can be baked a week in advance and frozen. To freeze, cool puffs completely on wire racks. Place in large zip-top freezer bags; seal tightly. Place bags in freezer. To recrisp puffs, thaw at room temperature. Place puffs on ungreased baking sheets. Bake at 400° for 5 minutes; cool completely before filling with Eggnog Pastry Cream.

Fix it Faster: If you don't have time to build this tree, just pile some puffs on individual dessert plates. (See photo on page 131.)

eggnog pastry cream

Prep: 4 min. **Cook:** 42 min. **Other:** 8 hrs.

¾ cup all-purpose flour
3 cups refrigerated eggnog
7 egg yolks
1½ tablespoons butter, softened
1½ teaspoons rum extract
1½ teaspoons vanilla extract

Place flour in a heavy saucepan; gradually whisk in eggnog until blended and smooth. Add egg yolks, 1 at a time, whisking until just combined after each addition.

Cook over medium-low heat, stirring constantly, until thickened (about 42 minutes). Remove from heat; stir in butter and extracts. Transfer pastry cream to a bowl. Cover surface with plastic wrap; chill 8 hours or overnight. (Pastry cream will be very thick.) **Yield:** 3½ cups.

Edible Tree Tips: Allow 45 minutes to build this edible tree and then at least 30 minutes in the refrigerator for it to firm up or 1 hour at room temperature before serving. If you chill it, you may need to temporarily remove a refrigerator shelf in order for the tree to fit.

Appetizers with Appeal

Each of these hors d'oeuvres is either make ahead or quick & easy—or both.

Asian Curry Dip

❄️*make ahead • quick & easy*

Asian Curry Dip

This spicy dip is great served with store-bought sweet potato chips, raw vegetables such as sugar snap peas, or boiled shrimp.

Prep: 6 min.   Other: 30 min.

½   cup sour cream
2   tablespoons seasoned rice vinegar
1   tablespoon soy sauce
1   tablespoon honey
1   teaspoon curry powder
1   teaspoon grated fresh ginger
1   teaspoon dark sesame oil
¼   teaspoon ground red pepper

Whisk together all ingredients in a small bowl. Cover and chill at least 30 minutes. Yield: ¾ cup.

Note: We tested with Terra exotic vegetable chips as dippers.

❄️*make ahead • quick & easy*

Smoked Salmon Spread

Serve this creamy spread with bagel chips or endive leaves.

Prep: 15 min.   Other: 1 hr.

2   (8-ounce) packages cream cheese, softened
2   (4-ounce) packages smoked salmon, coarsely chopped
⅔   cup chopped red onion
2   tablespoons chopped fresh dill or 2 teaspoons dried dill
1½ to 2 teaspoons freshly ground pepper
½   teaspoon grated lemon rind
1   tablespoon caper juice (from a jar of capers) or fresh lemon juice
Garnish: finely chopped red onion
Capers

Process cream cheese and salmon in a food processor until smooth, stopping to scrape down sides. Add ⅔ cup red onion and next 4 ingredients; process just until combined, stopping to scrape down sides. Transfer spread to a bowl. Cover and chill at least 1 hour. Garnish, if desired. Serve capers as an accompaniment. Yield: 3⅓ cups.

❄️*make ahead*

Reuben Cheese Ball

This cheese ball combines the flavors of a Reuben sandwich into the perfect party appetizer. Make the cheese mixture ahead, and roll in breadcrumbs just before serving. Spread leftovers on a sandwich.

Prep: 45 min.   Cook: 11 min.   Other: 1 hr.

1   (8-ounce) package cream cheese, softened
⅓   cup sour cream
2   cups (8 ounces) shredded Swiss cheese
1   cup (4 ounces) shredded extra-sharp Cheddar cheese (do not use preshredded)
1   cup chopped deli corned beef (6 ounces sliced)
¼   cup chopped sauerkraut, drained and squeezed dry
1   tablespoon spicy brown mustard
1   teaspoon caraway seeds, crushed
2   (1-pound) loaves party pumpernickel or rye bread
1   teaspoon butter or margarine, melted
¼   cup chopped fresh Italian parsley

Combine cream cheese and sour cream in a large bowl; beat at medium speed with an electric mixer until smooth. Add Swiss cheese and next 5 ingredients; beat at low speed until blended. Cover and chill 1 hour.

Process enough bread slices (about 3 or 4) to make ½ cup crumbs. Combine crumbs and melted butter; spread crumbs on a jellyroll pan. Bake at 350° for 5 to 6 minutes or until toasted. Cool completely. Combine toasted breadcrumbs and chopped parsley.

Shape chilled cheese mixture into a ball; roll in breadcrumbs and parsley. Cover cheese ball, and chill briefly until ready to serve.

Arrange remaining bread slices on a baking sheet; bake at 350° for 5 minutes or until toasted. Serve with cheese ball. Yield: 20 servings.

Sugar and Spice Pecans

Sugar and Spice Pecans

make ahead • quick & easy

Marinated Goat Cheese and Pine Nuts

This colorful make-ahead marinated cheese is ideal for entertaining. See photo on page 131.

Prep: 13 min.   Other: 3 hrs., 30 min.

1   (8-ounce) jar dried tomatoes in oil with herbs
Olive oil
2   garlic cloves, minced
2   tablespoons chopped fresh rosemary or
     2 tablespoons dried rosemary
1   teaspoon grated lemon rind
½   teaspoon dried crushed red pepper
½   teaspoon freshly ground black pepper
3   (3-ounce) packages goat cheese
¼   cup pine nuts, toasted

Drain tomatoes, reserving oil. Add enough olive oil to measure ¾ cup oil. Chop enough tomatoes to yield ½ cup; reserve remaining tomatoes for other uses.

Combine oil, tomatoes, garlic, and next 4 ingredients in a small bowl.

Using a sharp knife, carefully slice goat cheese in ¼"-thick slices. Place cheese in an 11" x 7" dish; pour marinade over cheese. Cover and chill several hours. Place marinated cheese on a serving platter; pour marinade over cheese, and sprinkle with pine nuts. Serve with crackers. Yield: 8 servings.

make ahead • gift idea

Sugar and Spice Pecans

Package these coated pecans in little gift bags, or set them out as hors d'oeuvres at a holiday gathering.

Prep: 5 min.   Cook: 45 min.

1   cup sugar
2   teaspoons pumpkin pie spice
2   teaspoons grated orange rind
¼   teaspoon salt
2   egg whites
¼   cup butter, melted
4   cups pecan halves

Stir together first 4 ingredients.

Beat egg whites at high speed with an electric mixer until foamy. Gradually add sugar mixture, beating at high speed until soft peaks form. Fold in melted butter and pecan halves. Spread coated nuts in a single layer on a large jellyroll pan lined with nonstick aluminum foil or parchment paper.

Bake at 250° for 45 minutes or until nuts are toasted, stirring every 15 minutes. Remove from oven; let cool completely on pan. Remove from pan. Store in an airtight container up to 2 weeks. Yield: 4 cups.

Pizza Bread

❄️ *editor's favorite • make ahead*
Red Pepper-Ham Roll-Ups

Get a jump on your holiday party food; make and freeze these rolls up to 1 month ahead. Slice frozen roll-ups, and let them thaw before serving.

Prep: 20 min.   Other: 20 min.

1	(8-ounce) package cream cheese, softened
1	(3-ounce) package cream cheese, softened
2	garlic cloves, finely chopped
⅓	cup finely chopped walnuts, toasted
¼	cup pitted kalamata or pimiento-stuffed olives, chopped
¼	cup roasted red bell peppers from a jar, patted dry and chopped
¼	teaspoon pepper
8	(⅛"-thick) slices premium deli ham (we tested with Boar's Head Black Forest Ham)
54	pitted kalamata olives

Beat cream cheese at medium speed with an electric mixer until creamy; stir in garlic and next 4 ingredients.

Spread about 2 tablespoons cream cheese mixture over each ham slice. Roll up, jellyroll fashion, starting with the long side. Place roll-ups, seam side down, on a baking sheet. Fill ends of rolls with remaining cream cheese mixture. Cover and freeze roll-ups 20 minutes.

Meanwhile, place olives on small wooden picks.

Using a sharp knife, slice each roll-up into 1" pieces; secure each with 1 olive pick. Cover and chill until ready to serve. Yield: about 4½ dozen.

Red Pepper-Ham Roll-Ups

❄️ *quick & easy*
Pizza Bread

Add your favorite toppings to these kid-friendly pizzas. We liked using both green and black olives.

Prep: 7 min.   Cook: 15 min.

1	(16-ounce) package twin French bread loaves (we tested with Pepperidge Farm)
1	(8-ounce) package cream cheese, softened
2	tablespoons mayonnaise
1	teaspoon dried Italian seasoning
1	(3.5-ounce) package pepperoni slices, chopped (we tested with Hormel)
1	(2¼-ounce) can sliced ripe olives or ½ cup pimiento-stuffed olives, sliced, or both
1	cup (4 ounces) shredded mozzarella cheese

Slice bread loaves in half horizontally.

Combine cream cheese, mayonnaise, and Italian seasoning in a small bowl; stir well. Spread evenly over cut sides of bread; sprinkle evenly with pepperoni and olives. Top with cheese. Place on a baking sheet. Bake at 375° for 12 to 15 minutes or until lightly browned. Cut each loaf half into 12 slices. Yield: 4 dozen appetizers.

❄*make ahead • quick & easy*
Smoked Sausage Bundles

Prep: 15 min.   Cook: 19 min.

1   (16-ounce) package fully cooked smoked sausage
2   (17.3-ounce) packages frozen puff pastry sheets, thawed
½   cup honey mustard dressing (we tested with Naturally Fresh)
1   large egg, lightly beaten
1   tablespoon water
Additional honey mustard dressing

Slice sausage into 36 slices; set aside.

Cut pastry sheets into 36 (3") squares; spread center of each square with ½ teaspoon honey mustard dressing. Place 1 piece sausage on dressing. Bring edges of pastry together; press to seal. Place bundles on lightly greased baking sheets. Whisk together egg and water; brush over bundles.

Bake at 400° for 19 minutes or until golden. Remove from baking sheet to a serving platter. Serve with additional dressing, if desired. Yield: 3 dozen.

❄*make ahead • gift idea*
Cheese-Jalapeño Jelly Thumbprints

Adults will love this savory twist on the traditional thumbprint cookie.

Prep: 39 min.   Cook: 14 min.   Other: 1 hr., 5 min.

1   (8-ounce) block sharp white Cheddar cheese, shredded
⅓   cup butter, softened
⅓   cup freshly grated Parmesan cheese
1   egg yolk
1¼ cups all-purpose flour
¼   teaspoon ground red pepper
¼   teaspoon salt
1   cup toasted pecan halves, finely ground
⅓   cup jalapeño pepper jelly

Process first 4 ingredients in a food processor until blended. Add flour, ground red pepper, and salt; process until dough forms a ball, stopping often to scrape down sides. Shape dough into a disc; cover and chill 1 hour.

Let dough stand at room temperature 5 minutes. Shape dough into 1" balls; roll in ground pecans.

Place balls 1" apart on ungreased baking sheets. Press thumb in center of each ball to make an indention.

Bake at 400° for 14 minutes or until browned. Immediately fill each center with a heaping ¼ teaspoon jelly, pressing gently into cookie with back of spoon. Remove from pans to wire racks; cool completely. Store in an airtight container between layers of wax paper up to 2 days. Yield: 3 dozen.

❄*make ahead*
Jalapeño-Sausage Cheese Squares

These spicy bites are great for a brunch buffet.

Prep: 8 min.   Cook: 42 min.   Other: 10 min.

1   pound hot or mild ground pork sausage
1   (12-ounce) jar pickled jalapeño slices, drained and patted dry
1½ (8-ounce) blocks Cheddar and Monterey Jack cheese, shredded
6   large eggs, lightly beaten
1   cup milk
1   teaspoon garlic powder
¼   teaspoon pepper

Cook sausage in a large skillet over medium-high heat, stirring until sausage crumbles and is no longer pink. Drain.

Place jalapeño slices in a lightly greased 13" x 9" baking dish. Top with sausage; sprinkle with cheese.

Whisk together eggs and next 3 ingredients. Pour over cheese.

Bake at 350° for 35 minutes or until set. Let stand 10 minutes. Cut into bite-size squares. Serve warm. Yield: about 4 dozen.

Note: To make this recipe ahead, bake as directed; let cool, cover, and chill up to 1 day. Reheat at 350° for 15 minutes; let stand briefly, and then cut into squares just before serving.

Bacon-Wrapped Shrimp
and Snow Peas

Bacon-Wrapped Shrimp and Snow Peas

Leave the tails on the shrimp if you're entertaining.

Prep: 18 min.   Cook: 12 min.   Other: 5 min.

1   tablespoon grated lime rind
2   tablespoons fresh lime juice
1   tablespoon dark sesame oil
1   teaspoon salt
½   to 1 teaspoon pepper
2   teaspoons hot sauce
12 jumbo shrimp, peeled (about ¾ pound)
12 fresh snow peas
12 fully cooked bacon slices (we tested with Armour
    Ready Crisp Bacon)

Toss together first 7 ingredients in a large bowl until shrimp are coated; let stand 5 minutes.

Trim ends of snow peas. Wrap each slice of bacon around 1 shrimp and 1 snow pea; secure with a wooden pick. Place shrimp on a lightly greased rack of a broiler pan. Repeat procedure with remaining shrimp, snow peas, and bacon.

Broil 3" from heat 12 minutes or until shrimp turn pink, turning after 6 minutes. Arrange appetizers on a serving platter. Serve hot. Yield: 6 appetizer servings.

Note: Use round rather than flat wooden picks; they're less likely to burn. Our secret to plump, pretty snow peas after baking is to first soak snow peas in a bowl of cold water 1 hour; then drain before skewering.

157

Food Gifts & Wrapping Ideas

Delight friends and family with heartfelt gifts from the kitchen, as well as some clever paper packaging. The recipes have secret shortcuts, and our wraps will make your gifts the snazziest selections under the tree.

Quick-Fix Food Gifts

Each of these recipes has a time-saving twist—we've added a homemade touch to purchased or packaged foods.

Marinated Cheese and Olives

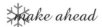
make ahead
Marinated Cheese and Olives

The shortcut here: dressing up cubed cheese and olives.

Prep: 5 min.   Other: 8 hrs.

- 4 (8-ounce) packages cubed colby-Jack cheese
- 1 (10-ounce) jar or 2 (7-ounce) jars kalamata olives, drained
- 1 (16-ounce) bottle olive oil and vinegar dressing
- 1 tablespoon dried Italian seasoning
- ½ teaspoon dried crushed red pepper
- 6 garlic cloves, crushed
- 6 fresh rosemary sprigs

Combine all ingredients except rosemary in a large bowl; stir gently. Cover and chill at least 8 hours or up to 24 hours.

Divide cheese and olives into 6 glass containers. Place 1 rosemary sprig in each container. Pour remaining dressing evenly into containers. Cover and refrigerate up to 2 weeks. Yield: 8 cups.

quick & easy • make ahead
Roasted Chili-Cheese Dip

We liked this dip served on tacos and burritos.

Prep: 17 min.   Cook: 8 min.

- 2 tablespoons butter or margarine
- ½ cup finely chopped sweet onion
- 2 large garlic cloves, minced
- 4 (8-ounce) containers refrigerated Mexican cheese dip (we tested with Olé)
- 1 (16-ounce) jar fire-roasted red and green chiles, drained and finely chopped (we tested with Melissa's)
- 1 teaspoon ground cumin

Melt butter in a large skillet over medium-high heat. Add onion; sauté 3 minutes or until tender. Add garlic; sauté 1 minute. Reduce heat to medium; stir in cheese dip, chiles, and cumin, stirring constantly until cheese melts. Serve warm with tortilla chips, or spoon dip into small jars or containers. Cover and chill. Give jars of dip as gifts along with reheating instructions. Yield: 5 cups.

Note: To reheat 1 cup dip, place in a microwave-safe bowl. Microwave dip on HIGH for 3 minutes, stirring after 1½ minutes.

Cheddar Cookies

This simplified cheese straw recipe uses self-rising flour, a food processor, and a cookie scoop to cut down on time. Look for a lever-release cookie scoop in specialty kitchen shops or large home-goods stores.

Prep: 24 min.   Cook: 12 min. per batch

- 2 cups self-rising flour
- ¾ cup cold butter, cut into pieces
- 1 (8-ounce) package shredded sharp Cheddar cheese
- ¾ teaspoon ground red pepper
- 3 tablespoons ice water

Toasted, salted pecan halves (optional; see Note)

Process flour and butter in a food processor until mixture resembles coarse meal. Add cheese and pepper; pulse 6 to 8 times or until combined. With processor running, gradually add water through food chute, and process just until dough forms a ball.

Drop dough by level tablespoonfuls 2" apart onto ungreased baking sheets. Flatten each cookie with the bottom of a glass; gently press 1 pecan half into center of each cookie, if desired.

Bake in batches at 400° for 12 minutes. Let cool on baking sheets 2 minutes. Remove cookies to wire racks to cool. Store in an airtight container. Yield: 4½ dozen.

Note: To toast pecan halves, coat them with cooking spray, and place in a large skillet. Cook over medium heat 6 to 7 minutes or until lightly toasted. Remove pecans to a paper towel, and sprinkle lightly with salt. Let cool.

Cheddar Cookies

Chocolate-Covered Cherry Cookies

Chocolate-Covered Cherry Cookies

Place these cookies in candy cups, and give them in a gift box.

Prep: 12 min. Cook: 10 min. per batch

⅓ cup butter, softened
⅓ cup shortening
1 large egg
1 (17.5-ounce) package chocolate chip cookie mix (we tested with Betty Crocker)
½ cup unsweetened cocoa
42 assorted chocolate-covered cherries (we tested with Russell Stover hand-dipped Cherry Cordials)
½ cup powdered sugar
4 to 5 teaspoons cherry liqueur or maraschino cherry juice

Beat butter and shortening in a large bowl at medium speed with an electric mixer until fluffy; add egg, beating until blended.
Combine cookie mix and cocoa; gradually add to butter mixture, beating well. Shape dough into 1" balls. Place balls 2" apart on ungreased baking sheets.

Bake at 375° for 8 to 10 minutes. Cool 2 minutes. Gently press 1 cherry candy in center of each cookie. Cool completely on baking sheets; transfer to wire racks.
Combine powdered sugar and liqueur in a small bowl, stirring until smooth. (Glaze should be thick, yet easy to drizzle.) Place glaze in a small zip-top plastic bag. Snip a tiny hole in 1 corner of bag. Drizzle glaze over cookies. Let stand until set. Yield: 3½ dozen.

Note: Depending on the size candy box you buy, you may need two boxes for these cookies.

Chocolate-Almond Croissants

Bakery-style croissants or frozen croissants work fine in this recipe. If using frozen croissants, slice them while frozen. See photo on page 159.

Prep: 28 min.   Cook: 7 min.   Other: 3 hrs.

1 (12½-ounce) can almond filling
1 dozen small croissants, split in half horizontally*
1 cup double chocolate morsels (we tested with Ghirardelli) or regular semisweet chocolate morsels
1 cup sliced almonds, toasted

Stir almond filling. Spread each croissant bottom with about 2 tablespoons almond filling. Cover with tops; place on a large foil-lined baking sheet, and bake at 325° for 7 minutes or until lightly toasted.
Place chocolate morsels in a small microwave-safe bowl; microwave on HIGH 1 to 2 minutes or until melted, stirring once. Spread melted chocolate over croissants. Sprinkle almonds over chocolate. Let stand at room temperature 2 to 3 hours or until chocolate is firm. Yield: 1 dozen.

*If you use frozen Sara Lee Petit French Style Croissants, you'll need 2 (6-ounce) packages.

Bittersweet Sugar Cookie Macaroons

Sandwich these coconut-covered sugar cookies together with chocolate. The shortcut: portioned cookie dough (see photo below).

Prep: 28 min. Bake: 13 min. per batch Other: 5 min.

1   (18-ounce) package refrigerated ready-to-bake sugar cookie bar dough (we tested with Nestlé)
3   cups sweetened flaked coconut
1   (4-ounce) bittersweet chocolate baking bar, chopped (we tested with Ghirardelli)
2   tablespoons whipping cream

Cut each cookie dough portion into 4 equal pieces. Roll dough pieces in coconut; shape into balls. Place balls 2" apart on lightly greased baking sheets.

Bake at 350° for 12 to 13 minutes or until edges are golden. Cool on baking sheets 5 minutes; transfer to wire racks to cool completely.

Combine chocolate and whipping cream in a small glass bowl. Microwave on HIGH 30 seconds; stir. Spoon melted chocolate into a small zip-top plastic bag. Snip a small hole in 1 corner of bag. Pipe ½ to 1 teaspoon chocolate mixture onto center of 40 cookie bottoms. Top with remaining half of cookies, pressing gently to adhere. Let sandwich cookies stand on wire racks for chocolate to harden. Yield: 40 sandwich cookies.

making macaroon sandwich cookies

▲ Cut each portion of cookie dough into four pieces.

▲ Pipe chocolate onto flat sides of half the baked cookies.

▲ Sandwich the chocolate with remaining cookies.

Chocolate-Raspberry Petits Fours

If additional frosting is needed, scrape off excess frosting from baking sheet, and reheat.

Microwave white chocolate morsels in a glass measuring cup on HIGH 1 minute or until melted, stirring after 30 seconds. Place white chocolate in a zip-top freezer bag. Snip a tiny hole in 1 corner of bag; drizzle melted white chocolate over brownies. Chill brownies 30 minutes or until chocolate is firm. Yield: 30 petits fours.

Note: Look for plastic flavor injectors in the kitchen gadget section at Wal-Mart.

Pistachio Pastry Twists

Wrap these flaky pastries in cellophane, and tie with ribbon, or deliver them in a vase. Add a monogram sticker to the vase to personalize the gift.

Prep: 28 min.   Cook: 19 min. per batch

2   egg yolks
1   tablespoon water
⅓   cup sugar
½   teaspoon ground cinnamon
½   teaspoon ground cardamom
1   (17.3-ounce) package frozen puff pastry sheets, thawed
½   cup finely chopped roasted pistachios
2   tablespoons butter or margarine, melted

Whisk together egg yolks and water in a small bowl. Combine sugar, cinnamon, and cardamom.

Carefully roll each sheet of puff pastry into a 9½" square on a lightly floured work surface. Brush each sheet with egg wash, and sprinkle with 2 tablespoons sugar mixture. Sprinkle chopped pistachios evenly over 1 sheet, leaving a ¼" border; top with remaining sheet, sugared side down. Firmly press edges to seal. Brush top of pastry with melted butter; sprinkle with remaining sugar mixture. Cut pastry into ¾"-thick strips, using a pizza cutter. Twist each strip 3 times, and place 2" apart on lightly greased baking sheets.

Bake at 400° for 19 minutes or until golden. Remove from pans immediately, and cool on wire racks. Yield: 10 twists.

Note: To reheat pastry twists, bake at 450° for 5 minutes or just until heated. Cool. (As they cool, they crisp up.)

❄️ make ahead
Chocolate-Raspberry Petits Fours

Place these moist little brownie bites in candy cups for gift giving.

Prep: 50 min.   Other: 30 min.

2   (11-ounce) boxes prebaked mini brownies (we tested with Entenmann's Little Bites Brownies)
⅓   cup seedless raspberry jam
1   tablespoon raspberry liqueur (optional)
1   (15-ounce) container pourable milk chocolate frosting (we tested with Betty Crocker)
½   cup white chocolate morsels

Place brownies on a wire rack set over a baking sheet.

Microwave jam in a glass measuring cup on HIGH 10 to 15 seconds or just until slightly melted; stir until smooth. Stir in liqueur, if desired. Pour a small amount of jam into a flavor injector; inject each brownie through the side with a small amount of jam. Refill injector as needed until all brownies are filled.

Microwave pourable frosting in original container on HIGH 20 seconds. Pour or spoon frosting over brownies.

Saffron and Golden Raisin Breakfast Bread

Saffron and Golden Raisin Breakfast Bread

Put your bread machine to work mixing this dough. We liked the bread best sliced and toasted.

Prep: 7 min.   Cook: 32 min.   Other: 2 hrs., 35 min.

¼   teaspoon saffron threads
2   teaspoons warm water
3   egg yolks
¾   cup warm water (75° to 85°)
2   tablespoons butter, softened
2   tablespoons granulated sugar
1   (12-ounce) package bread machine country white bread mix (we tested with Fleischmann's)
½   cup golden raisins
½   cup chopped walnuts
1   tablespoon water
Turbinado sugar

Combine saffron and 2 teaspoons water in a small bowl; let stand 5 minutes. Place saffron mixture, 2 egg yolks, ¾ cup warm water, and next 5 ingredients, including yeast packet from bread mix) in a bread machine. Set bread machine to "dough" setting according to manufacturer's instructions; start machine.

When dough cycle is complete, turn dough out onto a lightly floured surface, and knead several times. Form dough into a loaf, and place in a greased 9" x 5" loafpan. Let dough rise in a warm place (85°), free from drafts, for 1 hour or until doubled in size.

Combine remaining egg yolk with 1 tablespoon water. Brush tops of loaves with egg wash, and sprinkle with turbinado sugar.

Bake at 350° for 32 minutes or until golden. Remove from pan, and cool completely on a wire rack. Yield: 1 loaf.

Mini Breakfast Breads: Divide dough into 3 portions. Form into 3 small loaves, and place in 3 greased 5¾" x 3¼" loafpans. Continue with recipe, letting dough rise 40 minutes and baking mini loaves at 350° for 20 minutes or until golden. Yield: 3 loaves.

Note: We recommend cooling this loaf on its side on a wire rack. This helps the loaf maintain its shape.

Dried Tomato and Rosemary Flatbread

The key to crispy results here is rolling the dough out really thin.

Prep: 10 min.   Cook: 10 min.   Other: 5 min.

1   (6½-ounce) package pizza crust mix (we tested with Jiffy)
½   cup warm water (100° to 110°)
¼   cup minced dried tomatoes packed in oil, drained
2   tablespoons finely chopped fresh rosemary
Olive oil
2   tablespoons olive oil
½   cup (2 ounces) shredded Italian five-cheese blend

Combine first 4 ingredients in a medium bowl; stir well. Cover and let stand at room temperature 5 minutes. Turn dough out onto a heavily floured surface, and knead 1 minute or until dough forms a smooth ball, adding more flour, if necessary. Divide dough in half.

Roll each portion of dough into a 12" x 10" rectangle; transfer dough to 2 baking sheets brushed with olive oil. (To transfer dough easily, roll dough onto rolling pin, and unroll onto baking sheets.) Roll or press each portion of dough into a 14" x 12" rectangle. (Dough should be very thin.) Brush each portion with 1 tablespoon olive oil; sprinkle evenly with cheese.

Bake at 425° for 10 minutes or until crispy and cheese is browned. Remove flatbread to wire racks, and let cool completely. To serve, break flatbread into large pieces. Store in an airtight container. Yield: 6 to 8 servings.

Gingerbread Fruitcake

No one will guess that this brandy-soaked loaf starts with a cookie mix.

Prep: 12 min.   Cook: 1 hr.   Other: 40 min.

1   (7-ounce) package dried fruit bits (we tested with SunMaid)
¾   cup sweetened dried cranberries
6   tablespoons apricot brandy, divided
1   (14.5-ounce) package gingerbread cake and cookie mix (we tested with Betty Crocker)
1¼ cups water
1   large egg, lightly beaten
¾   cup chopped pecans, toasted

Combine dried fruit bits, cranberries, and ¼ cup brandy in a medium bowl. Let stand 30 minutes.

Place cake mix in a large bowl; make a well in center. Add water and egg, stirring just until blended. Stir in soaked dried fruit and chopped pecans. (Batter is not as thick as typical fruitcake batter.) Pour batter into a greased 9" x 5" loafpan.

Bake at 350° for 55 to 60 minutes or until a long wooden pick inserted in center comes out clean. Cool in pan on a wire rack 10 minutes; remove from pan. Poke holes in loaf at 1" intervals, using a long wooden pick. Brush remaining 2 tablespoons brandy over loaf. Cool completely on a wire rack. For best results, store in an airtight container 2 to 3 days before serving. Yield: 1 loaf.

make ahead
Creamy Chicken and Polenta Casserole

This recipe makes two casseroles. Keep one, and give the other to a friend, along with baking instructions.

Prep: 20 min.   Cook: 36 min.   Other: 10 min.

1   (32-ounce) container chicken broth
2   tablespoons butter or margarine
½   teaspoon freshly ground black pepper
1   cup yellow cornmeal
¾   cup shredded Parmesan cheese
1   (12-ounce) jar marinated quartered artichoke hearts, drained and coarsely chopped
1   (12-ounce) jar roasted red bell peppers, drained and chopped
4   cups shredded cooked chicken (about 1 large rotisserie chicken)
1   (16-ounce) jar roasted garlic Alfredo sauce (we tested with Classico)
⅓   cup chopped fresh basil
1½ cups (6 ounces) shredded Italian cheese blend

Bring first 3 ingredients to a boil in a large saucepan; gradually whisk in cornmeal. Cook 4 minutes or until thickened and bubbly, stirring constantly. Remove from heat; stir in Parmesan cheese. Spoon polenta evenly into 2 (8") square disposable ovenproof pans (see Note below). Cool 10 minutes.

Sprinkle artichoke hearts, peppers, and chicken evenly over polenta. Pour Alfredo sauce over chicken in both pans. Sprinkle with basil; top with Italian cheese blend. Cover and chill until ready to bake.

Before baking, place pan on center of a baking sheet. Bake, uncovered, at 350° for 25 minutes or until casserole is thoroughly heated. Yield: 2 casseroles (4 servings each).

Note: We tested with Glad OvenWare disposable pans. Clip and save instructions from back or bottom panel, and share these instructions when gift giving.

These festive
ingredients make an easy holiday fruitcake.

Brown Paper Packages

Add crafty trims for the cutest gifts under the tree.

Set Your Imagination Free

Search your sewing box and crafts drawer for nifty embellishments for kraft paper wrappings. Here, belt buckles cinch ribbons and a bandanna in place, and cording threads through a garland of jingle bells. A papier-mâché box (found at crafts stores) doesn't even require wrapping: Personalize the lid with a photo and spell out the recipient's name in block letters; then glue a ribbon around the edge for a fine finish.

There's nothing plain about brown paper wrappings when you glue, wire, tie, or stick on everything from buttons to cork circles.

Where to Find It

Source information is current at the time of publication; however, we cannot guarantee availability of items. If an item is not listed, its source is unknown.

page 2—cake pedestal: Pottery Barn; (888) 779-5176; www.potterybarn.com

page 5—wineglasses: Williams-Sonoma; (877) 812-6235; www.williams-sonoma.com; **flatware, ornaments, red napkin:** Pottery Barn; (888) 779-5176; www.potterybarn.com; **bowl:** Present Tense; (800) 282-7117; www.presenttense.com for a retailer near you

page 15—serving dish: Present Tense; (800) 282-7117; www.presenttense.com for a retailer near you

page 16—small serving dishes: *Southern Living At HOME®;* www.southernlivingathome.com for ordering information; **red ornament garland:** Christmas & Co.; Birmingham, AL; (205) 943-0020; www.christmasandco.com

page 19—plate: Lamb's Ears Ltd.; Birmingham, AL; (205) 969-3138 **ornament:** Christmas & Co.; Birmingham, AL; (205) 943-0020; www.christmasandco.com

page 25—mug: *Southern Living At HOME®;* www.southernlivingathome.com for ordering information

pages 26—dessert dishes: Pot Luck Studios; Accord, NY; (845) 626-2300; www.homeportfolio.com

page 27—serving dish: Bauer Pottery Company; (888) 213-0800; www.bauerla.com

page 28—white ironstone platter: Mulberry Heights; Birmingham, AL; (205) 972-1300

page 32—old ironstone bowl: Mulberry Heights; Birmingham, AL; (205) 972-1300

page 35—cake pedestal: The Zrike Company; Oakland, NJ; (201) 651-5158; **www.zrike.com**

page 38—cake pedestal: Attic Antiques; Birmingham, AL; (205) 991-6887

page 41—cake server: *Southern Living At HOME®;* www.southernlivingathome.com for ordering information; **cake plateau:** Christopher Glenn, Inc.; Birmingham, AL; (205) 870-1236

page 42—cake pedestal: Pottery Barn; (888) 779-5176; www.potterybarn.com

page 54—cake pedestal: Attic Antiques;

Birmingham, AL; (205) 991-6887

page 55—dishes, glasses, cone: Christine's; Mountain Brook, AL; (205) 871-8297; **ornaments:** Christmas & Co.; Birmingham, AL; (205) 943-0020; www.christmasandco.com; **mirror:** Tricia's Treasures; Homewood, AL; (205) 871-9779; **ribbon:** Midori, Inc.; (800) 659-3049; www.midoriribbon.com; **cake pedestal:** Pot Luck Studios; Accord, NY; (845) 626-2300; www.homeportfolio.com

pages 56–57—cherub wall basket: *Southern Living At HOME®;* www.southernlivingathome.com for ordering information; **ribbon:** Lamb's Ears Ltd.; Birmingham, AL; (205) 969-3138

page 58—wire basket: *Southern Living At HOME®;* www.southernlivingathome.com for ordering information

page 60—wire tray: *Southern Living At HOME®;* www.southernlivingathome.com for ordering information; **ornament:** Jan Barboglio; Dallas, TX; (214) 698-1920

page 61—pot: Smith & Hawken; (800) 940-1170; www.smithandhawken.com

page 63—copper pot: Pottery Barn; (888) 779-5176; www.potterybarn.com

page 65—dishes, glasses, cone: Christine's; Mountain Brook, AL; (205) 871-8297

page 66—chairs, bowl, candlesticks: King's House Antiques; Mountain Brook, AL; (205) 871-5787

pages 68–69—containers: King's House Antiques; Mountain Brook, AL; (205) 871-5787; **plates, flatware, glasses, napkins:** Table Matters; Mountain Brook, AL; (205) 879-0125; www.table-matters.com

pages 70–71—all items: King's House Antiques; Mountain Brook, AL; (205) 871-5787

page 72—decanters: Tricia's Treasures; Homewood, AL; (205) 871-9779; **bead garland:** Christine's; Mountain Brook, AL; (205) 871-8297

page 73—ornaments: Christmas & Co.; Birmingham, AL; (205) 943-0020; www.christmasandco.com;

mirror: Tricia's Treasures; Homewood, AL; (205) 871-9779; **ribbon:** Midori, Inc.; (800) 659-3049; www.midoriribbon.com; **cake pedestal:** Pot Luck Studios; Accord, NY; (845) 626-2300; www.homeportfolio.com

pages 74–75—candleholders: Seasons of Cannon Falls™ brand holiday and seasonal home accents are available in gift, specialty, and department stores across the country. To locate a retailer near you, please visit www.seasonsofcannonfalls.com and click on "Where to Shop," or call (800) 377-3335; **horse, urn on table, small picture frames, ornaments:** Henhouse Antiques; Birmingham, AL; (205) 918-0505; **glasses:** Lamb's Ears Ltd.; Birmingham, AL; (205) 969-3138; **dishes:** Pot Luck Studios; Accord, NY; (845) 626-2300; www.homeportfolio.com; **linens and candleholder:** Pottery Barn; (888) 779-5176; www.potterybarn.com

page 76—picture frame: Henhouse Antiques; Birmingham, AL; (205) 918-0505; **napkin:** Pottery Barn; (888) 779-5176; www.potterybarn.com; **angel:** Seasons of Cannon Falls™ brand holiday and seasonal home accents are available in gift, specialty, and department stores across the country. To locate a retailer near you, please visit www.seasonsofcannonfalls.com and click on "Where to Shop," or call (800) 377-3335.

page 77—napkins and candlesticks: Pottery Barn; (888) 779-5176; www.potterybarn.com

page 78—glasses and plates: Bromberg & Co.; (800) 633-4616; www.brombergs.com; **napkins:** Pottery Barn; (888) 779-5176; www.potterybarn.com; **pot for centerpiece:** Smith & Hawken; (800) 940-1170; www.smithandhawken.com

page 79—red flowerpot: Smith & Hawken; (800) 940-1170; www.smithandhawken.com; **pear stocking holder:** Pottery Barn; (888) 779-5176; www.potterybarn.com; **white pitchers:** Henhouse Antiques; Birmingham, AL; (205) 918-0505

pages 80–81—stocking and ornaments: Christmas & Co.; Birmingham, AL; (205) 943-0020; www.christmasandco.com;

trees and reindeer: Seasons of Cannon Falls™ brand holiday and seasonal home accents are available in gift, specialty, and department stores across the country. To locate a retailer near you, please visit www.seasonsofcannonfalls.com and click on "Where to Shop," or call (800) 377-3335.

pages 82–83—wooden vases, large red vases, lamp, furniture: At Home; Homewood, AL; (205) 879-3510;

ornaments, stockings, miniature pewter vases, red clear glass vases: Crate & Barrel; (800) 967-6696; www.crateandbarrel.com;

ornament stocking holders and napkin rings: Lamb's Ears Ltd.; Birmingham, AL; (205) 969-3138;

pillows, faux mink throw, red mercury votives: Pottery Barn; (888) 779-5176; www.potterybarn.com

pages 84–85—wooden vases and large red vases: At Home; Homewood, AL; (205) 879-3510;

ornaments, stockings, miniature pewter vases, red clear glass vases: Crate & Barrel; (800) 967-6696; www.crateandbarrel.com;

ornament stocking holders and napkin rings: Lamb's Ears Ltd.; Birmingham, AL; (205) 969-3138;

red mercury votives: Pottery Barn; (888) 779-5176; www.potterybarn.com

pages 86–87—chairs: Mulberry Heights; Birmingham, AL; (205) 972-1300;

candies: Hammond's Candies; (888) CANDY-99; www.hammondscandies.com;

gold ball ornaments: Henhouse Antiques; Birmingham, AL; (205) 918-0505; and Flora; Homewood, AL; (205) 871-4004;

china, candleholders, napkins: Pottery Barn; (888) 779-5176; www.potterybarn.com;

glasses and flower container: *Southern Living At HOME®;* www.southernlivingathome.com for ordering information

page 88—cake pedestals and cloche: Attic Antiques; Birmingham, AL; (205) 991-6887;

cookie and candy jars: Pottery Barn; (888) 779-5176; www.potterybarn.com; and Pier 1 Imports; (800) 245-4595; www.pier1.com

pages 90–91—candy and candy canes: Hammond's Candies; (888) CANDY-99; www.hammondscandies.com;

cake pedestal: Attic Antiques; Birmingham, AL; (205) 991-6887;

glass: *Southern Living At HOME®;*

www.southernlivingathome.com for ordering information

page 93—napkin: Lamb's Ears Ltd.; Birmingham, AL; (205) 969-3138;

pottery: Pottery Barn; (888) 779-5176; www.potterybarn.com

page 94—wire stocking: Christmas & Co.; Birmingham, AL; (205) 943-0020; www.christmasandco.com; and Seasons of Cannon Falls™ brand holiday and seasonal home accents are available in gift, specialty, and department stores across the country. To locate a retailer near you, please visit www.seasonsofcannonfalls.com and click on "Where to Shop," or call (800) 377-3335.

page 99—gift box: Lamb's Ears Ltd.; Birmingham, AL; (205) 969-3138

page 101—candles: Daedalus Candles; Birmingham, AL; (205) 871-1830; www.daedaluscandles.com

page 102—iron piece: *Southern Living At HOME®;* www.southernlivingathome.com for ordering information;

glass containers: Pottery Barn; (888) 779-5176; www.potterybarn.com

page 103—lanterns: Christopher Glenn, Inc.; Birmingham, AL; (205) 870-1236

pages 106–107—wire basket: Seasons of Cannon Falls™ brand holiday and seasonal home accents are available in gift, specialty, and department stores across the country. To locate a retailer near you, please visit www.seasonsofcannonfalls.com and click on "Where to Shop," or call (800) 377-3335.

page 108—red urn: Harmony Landing; Homewood, AL; (205) 871-0585; harmonylanding@aol.com

page 109—urn: *Southern Living At HOME®;* www.southernlivingathome.com for ordering information

page 111—flower container: Mulberry Heights; Birmingham, AL; (205) 972-1300

page 113—cards and Santa: Lamb's Ears Ltd.; Birmingham, AL; (205) 969-3138;

ornaments and stockings: A'Mano; Birmingham, AL; (205) 871-9093

page 114—cards: Lamb's Ears Ltd.; Birmingham, AL; (205) 969-3138; and Julia D. Azar Designs; Memphis, TN; for a retail store near you, visit the Web site www.juliadazar.com

page 115—Christmas tree card holders: Christmas & Co.; Birmingham, AL; (205) 943-0020; www.christmasandco.com;

cards: Julia D. Azar Designs; Memphis, TN;

for a retail store near you, visit the Web site www.juliadazar.com;

stockings: A'Mano; Birmingham, AL; (205) 871-9093

pages 116–117—stemless wineglasses: Williams-Sonoma; (877) 812-6235; www.williams-sonoma.com;

flatware, ornaments, red napkin: Pottery Barn; (888) 779-5176; www.potterybarn.com;

bowl: Present Tense; (800) 282-7117; www.presenttense.com for a retailer near you

page 118—bowl: Present Tense; (800) 282-7117; www.presenttense.com for a retailer near you

pages 119 and 122—stemless wineglasses: Williams-Sonoma; (877) 812-6235; www.williams-sonoma.com

page 120—soup tureen: Henhouse Antiques; Birmingham, AL; (205) 918-0505

page 123—platter: At Home; Homewood, AL; (205) 879-3510

page 128—cake pedestal: Lamb's Ears Ltd.; Birmingham, AL; (205) 969-3138

page 132—wooden board: *Southern Living At HOME®;* www.southernlivingathome.com for ordering information;

page 133—mug: The Zrike Company; Oakland, NJ; (201) 651-5158; www.zrike.com

page 137—serving plate: Present Tense; (800) 282-7117; www.presenttense.com for a retailer near you

page 147—cake pedestal: Annieglass; Watsonville, CA; (831) 761-2041

page 150—mugs: *Southern Living At HOME®;* www.southernlivingathome.com for ordering information;

ornament: Christmas & Co.; Birmingham, AL; (205) 943-0020; www.christmasandco.com

page 152—serving dish: Jan Barboglio; Dallas, TX; (214) 698-1920

page 155—serving dish (left): Jan Barboglio; Dallas, TX; (214) 698-1920

page 157—pedestal: Pot Luck Studios; Accord, NY; (845) 626-2300; www.homeportfolio.com

page 160—glass and forks: *Southern Living At HOME®;* www.southernlivingathome.com for ordering information

page 163—clear boxes: Organized Living; www.organizedliving.com

page 165—glass vase: Pottery Barn; (888) 779-5176; www.potterybarn.com

page 176—candy: Hammond's Candies; (888) CANDY-99; www.hammondscandies.com

Recipe Index

General Index

Contributors

Editorial Contributors:

Rebecca Boggan
Lauren Brooks
Jennifer Cofield
Lorrie Hulston Corvin
Lindsey Cunningham
Adrienne Davis
Caroline Grant
Susan Huff
Shannon Jernigan

Beth Jordan
Ana Kelly
Jeannie Lockard
Maloy Love
Andrea Nikolai
Frances Robinson
Katie Stoddard
Carole Sullivan
Jeannie Winford

Thanks to the following homeowners:

Carolyn and James Bradford
Kay and Eddie Clarke
Donna and William Davis
Kim and Robin Fipps
Sharon and Roy Gilbert
Judy and Bert Hill
Susan and Don Huff

Janice and John Hyche
Shannon and David Jernigan
Beth and Jimmy Jordan
Leigh Ann and Murray Ross
Katie and Tom Stoddard
Sandy and Jim Sparrow
Linda Wright

Thanks to these Birmingham businesses and organizations:

A' Mano
At Home Furnishings
Briarwood Presbyterian Church
Bromberg & Company
Christine's
Christmas & Co./FlowerBuds Inc.
The Cottage Shop
Daedalus Candles
Davis Wholesale Florist

Flora
Harmony Landing
Henhouse Antiques
King's House Antiques
Lamb's Ears Ltd.
Martin & Sons Wholesale Florist
Mulberry Heights
Table Matters
Tricia's Treasures

Special thanks:

Julia D. Azar Designs, Memphis, Tennessee
Seasons of Cannon Falls ™, Cannon Falls, Minnesota
Sugar Mountain Wreath & Garland, Newland, North Carolina

holiday planner

This special section is dedicated to making your holiday merry and free of stress. Pencil in all of the season's parties and events on the big planning calendars, and jot down notes on the many helpful lists. It will seem that your holiday is virtually planned for you!

NOVEMBER

Sunday	Monday	Tuesday	Wednesday
		1	2
6	7	8	9
13	14	15	16
20	21	22	23
27	28	29	30

2005

Thursday	Friday	Saturday
3	4	5
10	11	12
17	18	19
Thanksgiving 24	25	26

seasonal essentials

Check this list to ensure that you'll have all the necessities on hand.

☐ Greeting cards
☐ Party invitations
☐ Stamps
☐ Wrapping paper
☐ Gift bags
☐ Tissue paper
☐ Tape
☐ Gift tags
☐ Bows and ribbons
☐ Seasonal fruits
☐ Nuts
☐ Baking ingredients
☐ Extra napkins/table
   linens/dish towels
☐ Candles
☐ Fresh greenery clippings
☐ Wreaths and garlands
☐ Tree stand
☐ Holiday lights

things to do

DECEMBER

Sunday	Monday	Tuesday	Wednesday
4	5	6	7
11	12	13	14
18	19	20	21
Christmas 25	26	27	28

2005

Thursday	Friday	Saturday
1	2	3
8	9	10
15	16	17
22	23	Christmas Eve 24
29	30	New Year's Eve 31

holiday-ready pantry

Stock up on these pantry staples, and you'll be ahead of the game.

- ☐ Coffee (regular, decaf, and flavored) and tea
- ☐ Wine and sodas
- ☐ Sweetened condensed milk
- ☐ Assorted nuts
- ☐ Semisweet morsels
- ☐ Baking chocolate
- ☐ Flaked coconut
- ☐ Canned broths
- ☐ Spices: ground allspice, cinnamon, cloves, ginger, and nutmeg
- ☐ Jams, jellies, preserves
- ☐ Eggnog
- ☐ Seasonal fresh herbs
- ☐ Cranberries
- ☐ Canned pumpkin
- ☐ Butter
- ☐ Frozen/refrigerated bread dough
- ☐ Whipping cream
- ☐ Hot chocolate makings
- ☐ Ice in freezer

things to do

10 easy holiday decorations

Decking your home for the holidays can be a fun and rewarding experience. Here are 10 ideas to get you started.

1. **Give your sofa** a seasonal makeover by replacing everyday pillows with Christmassy red ones.
2. **Create a holiday window** treatment by draping garland on the window frame. Finish by hanging a small wreath in the center.
3. **Design a shimmering centerpiece** by arranging several pillar candles on top of a cake stand.
4. **Purchase wooden letters** at a crafts store, and hot-glue evergreen sprigs to them. Use the letters to spell out words, such as *Peace* or *Noel*, on your holiday buffet table.
5. **Spray-paint pinecones** gold or silver and arrange them in a glass bowl for a season-long centerpiece.
6. **Add a glow** to any festive arrangement with votive candles in small glass containers in seasonal hues.
7. **Weave color into the tree** with wide ribbons. Cut the ribbons in 3- to 4-foot lengths, and wind them through the branches. Use wired ribbon for the most flexibility.
8. **Add miniature poinsettias** to the Christmas tree for a special party. Nestle the pots on sturdy branches; the blossoms will fill in any gaps in the greenery.
9. **Hang ornaments** with ribbons instead of wire hangers.
10. **Trim your tree** with pink, red, and white carnations in addition to traditional ornaments. Put the stems in water vials to keep them fresh. Hide the vials among the branches.

Decorating To-Do List

Make short work of your annual holiday decorating by organizing your needs and ideas on these lines.

Gather materials

from the yard ....

from around the house ....

from the store ....

Add holiday decorations

to the table ....

to the buffet ....

to the door ....

to the mantel ....

to the staircase ....

to the chandelier ....

other ....

mix-and-match holiday menus

These menu ideas are based on recipes in the book.

Christmas Brunch

Grapefruit Compote in Rosemary Syrup,
page 16

Coffee Lovers' Coffee Cake, page 18, or
Belgian Waffles with Eggnog Butter and
Orange Syrup, page 143

Scrambled eggs   Grits   Bacon

Orange juice   Coffee

Appetizer Open House

Grapefruit-Rosemary Daiquiris, page 13

Wine

Savory Kalamata Cheesecake Squares,
page 14

Florentine Artichoke Dip, page 15

Warm Brie with Pear Preserves, page 133

Bacon-Wrapped Shrimp and Snow Peas,
page 157

Sugar and Spice Pecans, page 154

Grapes

Holiday Dessert Party

Pecan Biscotti, page 24

Spiced Eggnog Pound Cake, page 144

Double Chocolate Espresso Brownies,
page 23

Caramel-Chocolate Tartlets, page 137

Rum Fudge Cakes, page 17

Peppermint Patty Hot Chocolate, page 133

Hazelnut-Eggnog Punch, page 141

Kids' Christmas Party

Roasted Chili-Cheese Dip, page 161

Florentine Artichoke Dip, page 15

Pizza

White Chocolate, Peanut, and Caramel Candy Cookies, page 23

Soft drinks   Milk

Seafood Night

Smoked Salmon Spread, page 153

Bacon-Wrapped Shrimp and Snow Peas, page 157

Grilled fish

Salad   Crusty bread

Wine or beer

Holiday Dinners

Seasoned Roast Turkey, page 30

Giblet Gravy, page 30

Grits Dressing, page 33

Cranberry sauce

Green Peas and Baby Limas with Pine Nuts, page 33

Roasted Sweet Potato Salad, page 32

Pecan pie

Holiday Fig Cake, page 36

Marinated Cheese and Olives, page 161

Creamy Chicken and Polenta Casserole, page 167

Green beans

Rosemary Roasted Grape Tomatoes, page 136

Cheesecake Swirl Bars, page 149

Tawny Baked Ham, page 29

Green Peas and Baby Limas with Pine Nuts,
page 33

Roasted Sweet Potato Salad, page 32

Dinner rolls

Hazel's Fresh Coconut Cake, page 40

Green salad

Pork Chops with Shallot-Cranberry Sauce,
page 136

Mashed potatoes

Green beans

Rosemary Roasted Grape Tomatoes,
page 136

Apple-Berry Cobbler with Vanilla Bean
Hard Sauce, page 27

Beet Salad with Curried Walnuts, page 31

Beef Tenderloin with Shallot Sauce, page 29

Grits Dressing, page 33

Green Peas and Baby Limas with Pine Nuts,
page 33

Sautéed carrots

Chocolate Tiramisù Charlotte, page 129

party planner

This handy chart helps you keep track of who's bringing what to the big holiday gathering.

guests	what they're bringing	serving pieces needed
	☐ appetizer ☐ beverage ☐ bread ☐ main dish ☐ side dish ☐ dessert	
	☐ appetizer ☐ beverage ☐ bread ☐ main dish ☐ side dish ☐ dessert	
	☐ appetizer ☐ beverage ☐ bread ☐ main dish ☐ side dish ☐ dessert	
	☐ appetizer ☐ beverage ☐ bread ☐ main dish ☐ side dish ☐ dessert	
	☐ appetizer ☐ beverage ☐ bread ☐ main dish ☐ side dish ☐ dessert	
	☐ appetizer ☐ beverage ☐ bread ☐ main dish ☐ side dish ☐ dessert	
	☐ appetizer ☐ beverage ☐ bread ☐ main dish ☐ side dish ☐ dessert	
	☐ appetizer ☐ beverage ☐ bread ☐ main dish ☐ side dish ☐ dessert	
	☐ appetizer ☐ beverage ☐ bread ☐ main dish ☐ side dish ☐ dessert	
	☐ appetizer ☐ beverage ☐ bread ☐ main dish ☐ side dish ☐ dessert	
	☐ appetizer ☐ beverage ☐ bread ☐ main dish ☐ side dish ☐ dessert	
	☐ appetizer ☐ beverage ☐ bread ☐ main dish ☐ side dish ☐ dessert	
	☐ appetizer ☐ beverage ☐ bread ☐ main dish ☐ side dish ☐ dessert	
	☐ appetizer ☐ beverage ☐ bread ☐ main dish ☐ side dish ☐ dessert	
	☐ appetizer ☐ beverage ☐ bread ☐ main dish ☐ side dish ☐ dessert	
	☐ appetizer ☐ beverage ☐ bread ☐ main dish ☐ side dish ☐ dessert	
	☐ appetizer ☐ beverage ☐ bread ☐ main dish ☐ side dish ☐ dessert	

Guest List

Keep a record of names, addresses, and phone numbers of whom
you plan to invite to your holiday festivities.

Pantry List

Make an inventory of what you have and
what you need.

Party To-Do List

Create a list to refresh your memory
as partytime approaches.

Christmas dinner details
Organize the feast by making notes on these pages. Keep our table-setting tips handy for quick reference every time you entertain.

Setting a Proper Place

Follow these guidelines to make the table a welcoming place to enjoy the season's most important meal.

• **Add color and warmth with a tablecloth or place mats,** or place the dinner plate and charger right on the table.

• **Position the napkin to the left of the place setting.** If food is served family style or filled plates are brought from the kitchen after family and friends are seated, you can place the napkin in the center of the charger or place mat.

• **Arrange the charger or dinner plate 1 inch from the edge of the table.** Position the flatware pieces beginning at the outside edge according to their order of use. Place the **knife,** with the blade turned toward the plate, on the right side of the plate. Set the **spoons** to the right of the knife; position the **soup spoon** to the extreme right. Set the **forks** on the plate's left, beginning at the outside edge according to their logical sequence: salad fork and then meat or dinner fork. Bring in the **dessert fork or spoon** with dessert.

• **Place the water glass above the knife.** If you're serving iced tea or wine, set the appropriate glass to the right of the water glass above the spoon.

• **If soup or salad is served as a separate course, place the individual bowl or plate on the charger.** If salad is served with the meal, position the salad plate or bowl on the left side by the fork.

• **If the entrée is served with a sauce or gravy, consider using a separate small plate for bread and butter.** Place the bread-and-butter plate above the forks. When using a butter spreader, rest the spreader at the top of the bread plate parallel to the table's edge with the handle to the right.

• **When serving coffee or tea with a meal, place the cup and saucer to the right of the spoons.** If served with dessert, bring in the cup and saucer at that time.

Guest List

Write your Christmas dinner invitation list. Include addresses and phone numbers.

....

....

....

....

....

....

....

....

....

....

....

....

....

....

....

....

....

Menu Ideas

Note recipes from the past that went over well, as well as new ideas for this season.

....
....
....
....
....
....
....
....
....
....
....
....
....
....
....

Dinner To-Do List

Write your list and check It twice for a no-stress meal.

....
....
....
....
....
....
....
....
....
....
....
....
....
....
....

gifts and greetings
Use these pages to note everyone on your Christmas card and gift lists this year. The size charts ensure that every gift fits perfectly.

Christmas Card List

name	address	sent/received

Gift List & Size Charts

name ....

jeans_____ shirt_____ sweater_____ jacket_____ shoes_____ belt_____

blouse_____ skirt_____ slacks_____ dress_____ suit_____ coat_____

pajamas_____ robe_____ hat_____ gloves_____ ring_____

name ....

jeans_____ shirt_____ sweater_____ jacket_____ shoes_____ belt_____

blouse_____ skirt_____ slacks_____ dress_____ suit_____ coat_____

pajamas_____ robe_____ hat_____ gloves_____ ring_____

name ....

jeans_____ shirt_____ sweater_____ jacket_____ shoes_____ belt_____

blouse_____ skirt_____ slacks_____ dress_____ suit_____ coat_____

pajamas_____ robe_____ hat_____ gloves_____ ring_____

name ....

jeans_____ shirt_____ sweater_____ jacket_____ shoes_____ belt_____

blouse_____ skirt_____ slacks_____ dress_____ suit_____ coat_____

pajamas_____ robe_____ hat_____ gloves_____ ring_____

name ....

jeans_____ shirt_____ sweater_____ jacket_____ shoes_____ belt_____

blouse_____ skirt_____ slacks_____ dress_____ suit_____ coat_____

pajamas_____ robe_____ hat_____ gloves_____ ring_____

name ....

jeans_____ shirt_____ sweater_____ jacket_____ shoes_____ belt_____

blouse_____ skirt_____ slacks_____ dress_____ suit_____ coat_____

pajamas_____ robe_____ hat_____ gloves_____ ring_____

name ....

jeans_____ shirt_____ sweater_____ jacket_____ shoes_____ belt_____

blouse_____ skirt_____ slacks_____ dress_____ suit_____ coat_____

pajamas_____ robe_____ hat_____ gloves_____ ring_____

name ....

jeans_____ shirt_____ sweater_____ jacket_____ shoes_____ belt_____

blouse_____ skirt_____ slacks_____ dress_____ suit_____ coat_____

pajamas_____ robe_____ hat_____ gloves_____ ring_____

holiday memories

Write the season's best moments on these pages to preserve them for years to come.

Treasured Traditions

Whether you started a new one or made improvements to an old one, capture
your favorite holiday traditions on these lines.

Special Holiday Events

Make a list of the dates and times of the plays, concerts, and events you want to attend this year.
You can even use this space to start your list for next year.

Holiday Visits & Visitors

Keep a record of family and friends who shared the season with
you. Jot down updates, such as marriages and births.

This Year's Favorite Recipes

Appetizers and Beverages ....

Entrées ....

Sides and Salads ....

Cookies and Candies ....

Desserts ....

notes for next year

Favorite Things

Use this space as a journal to keep your impressions of Christmas 2005 fresh year-round.

Get a Head Start

Once Christmas 2005 is a pleasant memory, make notes about what you want to change or repeat for Christmas 2006.